CHARLES MENDLOWICZ

the sincere economist

18 PRINCIPLES TO HELP YOU EVOLVE

WHY YOU WERE BORN TO REACH YOUR FULL POTENTIAL

18 principles to help you evolve

The contents of this book are the sole responsibility of the author and do not necessarily reflect the views of the publisher.

ISBN: 978-1-64095-654-4
Ebook ISBN: 978-1-64095-655-1

Editorial production and distribution:

contato@citadel.com.br
www.citadel.com.br

Distributed in English language by:

SOUND WISDOM

P.O. Box 310 • Shippensburg, PA 17257-0310 • 717-530-2122
info@soundwisdom.com

CHARLES
MENDLOWICZ
the sincere economist

EVOLVE

WHY YOU WERE BORN TO REACH YOUR FULL POTENTIAL

2023

Contents

P

Prologue

Sometimes the world doesn't "break" you on the spot, it gradually wears you down to the point where you feel paralyzed or lost. At such times, routine and discipline are the best antidotes to get you back into the "game" and rediscover the path to your EVOLUTION.

The year in which everything definitely went wrong for me was 2013. For the first time in my life - in which I believed everything was fine, because I had stability, had always been successful professionally and was in a solid, long-term relationship - I felt lost. I found myself not knowing exactly what to do; I already knew what I didn't want, but I wasn't clear on what I was going to do from then on.

When you don't know what you're going to do with your life because you're lost, don't want to work or don't want to study, there really isn't much to do. Now, when you don't know what you want to do after you've had a brilliant career and a lot of money and built something, the process of coming to terms with it all becomes even more difficult. After all, those who have always been lost usually live well with this reality. But when you've already achieved something, what happens next?

I was excited at the start of 2013. I decided it was time to invest in an old dream linked to my passion for cooking and wine, so I embarked on a six-month professional boulangerie and sommelier training course in Curitiba, about an hour and a half from where I lived, in Joinville, Santa Catarina. But, Charles, what do you mean? Aren't you an economist? Calm down, this will all make sense.

I had just spent the previous fourteen years working uninterruptedly in the financial and retail market, becoming commercial superintendent of one of the largest financial companies at the time, between 1998 and 2008, where I started as a trainee. I then went on to become commercial coordinator and then manager of one of the largest drinks companies in the world - yes, Coca-Cola. I got to know more than a thousand businesses throughout Brazil, made a lot of money, accumulated a series of qualifications in my field (including two MBAs at good institutions, as well as teaching at two universities) and thousands of hours of work, living in a constant operational loop that for a long time also served as a shield.

Everything seemed to be fine, the way I had always faced life, even though I had accumulated a generous 130 kilos that made me very tired, as well as carrying some health problems derived from a life of excessive work, chronic lack of exercise and that basic binge eating that was part of the package of self-destruction that we almost never realize we take home at certain times in our lives, or sometimes throughout it. But when 2011 arrived, along came the first and biggest seismic tremors of my journey, and that's how I began to force myself to wake up.

That year marked my departure from Coca-Cola, where I had been growing a lot, and that was the first point that gave me that general shake-up, but I still decided to move on. I even received invitations to return to the financial market as soon as I left the company, but I didn't feel comfortable with the idea after becoming disillusioned with some of the things I saw and knew how they worked; I couldn't stand it any longer.

Then, when I realized that the situation was getting even more serious, to the point of admitting to myself that I didn't want to work in either banking or drinking anymore, the restlessness to become an entrepreneur arose. "That's it, I'm starting a new business!" Motivated by my passion for cooking, I clung to this thought and started 2013 already using the resources I had applied over the last few years to put the plan to specialize in boulangerie into practice. After all, although I loved making brownies, cakes and pies, it wasn't a subject I had mastered professionally to the point of starting a business in the area.

Then you think: new year, new life. Seriously, I really wanted to believe that, but do you know what it's like not to have time to taste the change? That's exactly what happened to me throughout 2013. In the months that followed, the tremors began to get more and more intense until the floor of my entire world opened up. If you've ever experienced back-to-back losses or know someone who has, you'll understand how this can drive you to the brink of madness.

⌘

March 2013. All I remember is that I arrived in a hurry, flying from Curitiba to Rio just in time to say goodbye to my grandfather, Norberto Mendlowicz, also known as Seu Norberto, who had been battling cancer for the last few months. My grandfather was my father, as my biological father had left us when I was very young. If it hadn't been for Grandpa Norberto, a typical Jew who fled to Brazil before the Second World War, I wouldn't have had a father figure who simply taught me most of the things I know. Until I was in my early twenties, my grandfather pushed me hard to be someone in life; amid all the hustle and bustle of everyday life, Sunday snacks at my grandmother Cyrla Mendlowicz's (Dona Celina) house were our meeting point. We would spend hours chatting, as he was always very interested in everything I did. "What's up, Charles? Are you hitting your quotas?" he would ask me about my work targets. My conciliatory manner, which anyone who knows me knows I have, came from him, as did my love of living and thriving in life. He was an incredible guy, with a whole life dedicated to family, charity and work.

Today I still have a hard time remembering his departure, because at that moment I once again allowed the steamroller that had been my life to run over everything and soon put me into automatic mode. After the funeral, I went back to Curitiba to continue the training I had just started.

⌘

I really wanted to get back to my routine and convince myself that everything was all right again; however, as that year didn't come into my life for nothing, shortly afterwards death came back to haunt me.

Scabuska was six years old, with no health problems and following his normal life as a dog. He loved his kennel, as Patrícia and I had work commitments that took us away from home for long periods of time. One fine day, they called us from there: "You need to come running, he's not well".

We didn't have time to do much. A few days later we lost our Golden Retriever, whom we had practically taken for a son, without much explanation as to why it had happened; all we knew was that it was a fulminant illness. My greatest pain is that in previous years I had spent little time with him; in just a few months we would have been together every day, but there was no time. He was taken away from me. In March I lost my grandfather and, in May, my dog - who, believe me, laughed when he met me...

Man, it was heavy. I could feel the imbalance consuming me more and more around the edges. It didn't seem possible to make everything I'd been feeling since the loss of my grandfather any worse. So once again I silenced the pain and just carried on. I needed to move on. The course and the idea of starting a business were there to keep me focused and not stop. I had no idea what to do if I stopped to think about what was happening.

When we finally reached the middle of 2013, for the first time I was able to feel truly happy when I heard: "Baby, I'm pregnant! We did it!". That was it! That dark tide was over; I was finally going to realize my great dream of being a father!

We had already lost two other pregnancies (2010 and 2011), and this was the third time my wife had been pregnant. We wanted it very much, we always had. But in August 2013, another bombshell hit: we lost our third child. I became a son without a father, and a father without children, all at the same time. I lost a father (grandfather), a dog and a son.

These are the moments that make you doubt everything, and it was no longer possible for me to use my routine as an excuse not to face up to what was happening to me. My grandfather, who was my father figure and an incredible person; my dog, who died with no logical explanation; my son, who I didn't get the chance to meet for the third time in a row. Why had I simply lost everything in such a short space of time?

In August, I had completed my training in boulangerie and sommelier, but the truth was that I no longer saw any point in much of what I was doing. Then one day, while watching TV, my memory took me back to an experience I had in 2008, when I did an exchange program in South Africa to improve my English; it turned out to be a very transformative experience, which marked the end of a cycle in my life.

"Why don't I travel again?" I thought. I wanted to find a way out of the situation I was in before I went mad, and of course, if you look you find. That's how I started researching itineraries that very day; and you know those advertisements that just seem random, popping up on the sides of your search page? I found my destination.

"Santiago de Compostela... sounds nice," I said to myself. I always tell people not to research the Camino de Santiago de Compostela, because if they do, this place will suck them in, and it was no different for me. I started researching and soon found movies, documentaries, books, and as soon as I'd finished watching all these things, I felt: "I need to go there".

It was late August, almost September, and the Camino de Santiago de Compostela practically closes in November for climatic reasons - it starts snowing a lot in the region and the crossing becomes impossible - meaning that I would either go in October or not until the following year. So, with less than two months to go, no experience whatsoever in the subject and zero physical preparation to face the eight hundred kilometers of the route, I bought the ticket, a backpack, a pair of boots and a staff that very same day; then I told my wife what I was about to do.

I did something crazy, because the normal thing for anyone who decides to embark on a journey like this is to prepare at least two or three years in advance, study the route, research what to do, and not just go out and buy a backpack and a pair of boots and then set off down the road like I did.

It's hard to explain. Although it seemed like an escape, in reality I just felt like I had to leave where I was and go somewhere else. What's more, the whole thing was challenging because it involved so many factors. A curious fact is that for many the path is a Christian religious route, and I'm Jewish. But the path is inclusive of everyone who is looking to make a process of atonement, which is ultimately what I went to do, without knowing, in the end, that it also involved this.

I needed to get it all out, and the Charles who left wasn't the same one who came back.

October 25, 2013. After arriving at Madrid's Barajas airport, I grabbed my suitcase in a hurry; the train was about to leave and I couldn't (or shouldn't) be tired the next day.

I needed to get to Saint-Jean-Pied-de-Port, a French village at the foot of the Pyrenees, where I would begin a journey on foot to cross all of Spain on the almost eight hundred kilometers of the Camino de Santiago de Compostela. I only had a little information, but I knew that the first day would be the toughest, with 21 kilometers of ascent and another six kilometers of descent, crossing the border between France and Spain along Napoleon's route.

Everything was rushed and confusing for someone who wasn't prepared (zero preparation at all) for it. In reality, I was destroyed, totally destroyed, physically and emotionally.

I grew up with Rocky Balboa's motto ("It doesn't matter how hard you hit, it's how much you can take and keep going"), and until 2013 I managed to fight back, get hit and get up. I just kept going; I managed to study, work, grow and earn more money than I ever imagined I could. But 2013 came devastatingly, and I couldn't resist.

I

Introduction

Madness. That's how I define it when we have our purpose right in front of us, but we don't do what we came here to do.

There came a time in my life when I started working with food, wine, a whole host of random things, when in reality, since I was young, I've always liked the same two subjects: economics and technology; especially technology and social networks, no wonder I had my BBS in 1994. However, I kept drifting away from my true passions (and I bet you've done the same).

The craziest thing is that I was one of the first guys to post a video on YouTube back in 2007; and you know what? Of my dog Scabuska, playing while he was still a puppy. YouTube had only just been created, and few Brazilians were uploading videos to the platform yet, and do you know why I was one of the first Brazilians to have an account on the channel, as well as one of the first on Orkut, Facebook and Instagram? Because I've always been a technology fanatic.

Now you're asking me: "OK, Charles, so why did you ignore it for so long?". In fact, I only started working with technology in 2017, but now, going back in time and analyzing all this, I realize that, in reality, for years and years I fought against what I really came to do in this world. I looked for a lot of things, but nothing moved. But that's also because they didn't really have to, because they weren't aligned with my purpose. On the other hand, I wouldn't be able to help people as I do today if I hadn't suffered a little, because I wouldn't understand them. For example, when someone comes to me and says they've lost money on the financial market, I know what they're talking about because I've been there. So from the moment I became aware of this question of purpose, I knew that I could no longer let other people spend as much time outside their purpose as I did.

Over the years I've been talking to people who come to me to talk about money and investments, I've realized that everyone wants to make money, everyone wants to change their lives, they want to have a better house, a better car, a better job, better household finances; but in my view, my personal and professional experience, if you don't change some fundamental things first, you won't be able to achieve any of this.

People want to start at the end, but we have to start at the beginning. So there's no point in talking about earning money, exchanging your 2007 Fiesta for a brand new one, or whether it's worth buying or financing an apartment in 420 months if you're not doing the basics, or rather, if you haven't even understood the basics yet. There's no point in wanting to earn something without living the process. In this formula, the math doesn't add up, because first you need to conquer the tools that will enable you to get to where you want to be.

In order to get somewhere, like those financial, career and life changes you're looking for, which I know you are, you'll need to follow a path; and everything I'm going to tell you here in this book, through eighteen basic principles, is nothing more than the trail that will take you towards the place you want to get to. That's not to say that this path is going to be smooth, so be prepared, because it's going to rain, it's going to be windy, it's going to be too sunny, but the good thing is that you'll finally have a path to follow.

During all the time I was off the path that led me to find my purpose, I went as far as to do something insane, like not living a whole year of my life in a minimally normal way. In 2008, I didn't stop working for the next 365 days. I had just been hired at a new company and was traveling all over Brazil for work, as well as studying for an MBA and traveling every weekend from Santa Catarina to Curitiba. I put on weight because I never paid attention to what I ate, I didn't even know what physical activity was; I didn't sleep properly because my head wouldn't take a break, already thinking about the next day's delivery, and soon my body began to show signs of breaking down, causing me to go to a pharmacy because I felt so sick when my blood pressure hit 18/10. It was as if I was on a bicycle that I couldn't stop pedaling or I'd fall off and break down. Without a shadow of a doubt, it was the craziest year of my life.

Then you ask me: "But why did you live like that, Charles? What was the point? In reality, I didn't even have time to think about whether everything I was doing was with the intention of building something, as in the story of sowing, in other words, planting and reaping, because I still wasn't clear about why I was doing all that and especially in that way, almost killing myself. But it's important to remember that many of the things I did contributed to my growth. Now I think it's clearer why I ended up on the Camino de Santiago de Compostela, because I literally wanted to find a direction in my life; the way out I found at the time was to live all the hardships of the middle of the road in concrete, to finally understand that if I didn't have a purpose for doing things, absolutely nothing would make sense, and I wouldn't be alive.

As I've told you several times, I'm Jewish. I grew up in Jewish culture under the influence of my grandparents, and was even literate in Portuguese and Hebrew as a child. I did my Bar Mitzvah, I attend synagogues whenever I can, and I have kept many of the principles of Judaism throughout my life, becoming perhaps one of the biggest practitioners in my family, although this was never an imposition in my upbringing. I talk about this subject calmly because at many times it has been my faith in God that has supported me, and I even say that if there are other lives, the only thing I would like to repeat would be to come with that same faith within my religion.

Not only did walking the Camino de Santiago change my life, but recognizing the principles that would guide it so that I could discover what I really had to do with my existence was the decisive turning point. The process of reflection I experienced during that journey made me feel again what I had been struggling to feel after all the beating I had taken over the last year. I felt "alive" again.

Life is the most important thing we have in this world, so much so that when I start my day, I always share stories with people on Instagram asking them if they've seen how beautiful it is outside and if they've "given thanks for another day of life". You yourself, who are reading this book of mine right now, have you ever paid attention to that? Have you ever thought that there will simply come a day when we all go to sleep and never wake up? Anything else in your life could be wrong, but if you're not alive, it's simply over.

When I realized that life is the most important thing we have, I understood even more the meaning of the word "chai", which in Hebrew means "alive". Not only does "chai" mean "alive", but its numerical counterpart is "eighteen", because of the words that form it, "Yod" (ten) and "Het" (eight). According to some rabbinic explanations, everything that is alive is in motion and in a constant process of evolution, and the number 18 concentrates all of this.

From this realization that everything is connected to this divine spark that is our own life, I finally understood that I had to follow some basic principles, which is what I've done over the last few years until I got to where I am right now, and also share them with everyone, because otherwise nothing would make sense.

I'll tell you one thing: if in my past I'd had the knowledge I'm going to share throughout this book, I would have followed my purpose much earlier and avoided suffering a lot of pain. You'll see that none of the 18 principles I'm going to describe are random; get ready to practice them one by one in your life from today onwards. Another important point is that I'm not asking you to do anything extreme, like walk barefoot on hot coals and risk burning the soles of your feet. I'm just asking you to give yourself a chance and try out a new route, a new path that will lead you to your best version, to your purpose.

All the people I've met in my life who are well-resolved and successful, just like me, have gone down this route.

So there's no point in looking for shortcuts. Enough of this bullshit! It's time to turn the key and change your life.

Come with me, trust Charlão and say goodbye to your fucked-up version.

I'll show you a path to a prosperous life.

Get ready, your EVOLUTION starts now.

Principle

The responsibility is all yours
(at least from now on)

I'll start this chapter by saying this: if you don't think you're responsible, you can close this book. "Damn, Charles, that's so ignorant," someone more sensitive might say in self-defense, but let me explain why I've just fired off this reality. If you don't think that responsibility lies with you, but with your mother, father, grandfather, husband, wife, fiancé or fiancée, if you depend on someone else to make your plans work, or blame someone else for your failure to evolve, there's no point in following the principles described in this book, because you believe that it doesn't lie with you, but with a third party.

Look, I'm going to make your life easier here, because in this principle of self-responsibility I explain that the responsibility is yours, at least from now on. Because if, before reading this book, you thought that your problem was because your father didn't give you professional support, ok, I forgive you. But from now on, there's no more thinking that it's everyone else's responsibility but yours. Otherwise, what's the point of me telling you what to do if your father still doesn't support you? We can only evolve when we understand that the burdens and bonuses depend solely on our responsibility and no one else's.

I've told the story I'm about to share with you elsewhere. When a Jew turns thirteen, he has a party called the Bar Mitzvah, and on that day a prayer must be said which has the important function of demonstrating that that Jewish child can already read and, from that moment on, has certain responsibilities. Over the years, this has helped the Jewish people a lot, because the children of other peoples still didn't know how to read; it contributed a lot to the cognitive development of the Jewish people, after all, it was a habit.

Well done. When it was my turn to go through the Bar Mitzvah, I had to learn this recitation; I had to study it, which usually takes about six months before the ceremony. I was twelve years old and I started studying, at that time on cassette tapes, and do you know how it worked? I had a prayer teacher, and we prayed together, me with that squeaky teenage male voice, a bit thick at one point and thin at another, something really awful, but she would teach me the prayer and I would record the cassette and take it home. In the next class, I had to show that I had learned to sing the prayer. In the very first class, we went there and prayed, the teacher gave me the tape; in the next class, when I entered the room, she asked: "Did you study the prayer?" Half trembling, I replied: "No". When I tried to explain, she cut me off by saying: "Look, I don't care if Dad's sick, if Mom couldn't work, if your puppy got sick. If you haven't studied, you can leave". I tried to say something right then and there to avoid being put in that situation, but she was fulminating: "No, no. You can leave. You can leave. It's fine with me, because I already know how to pray. But when the day of your party comes, it's you who has to know how to pray, not me".

What was the result? Do you think I learned to pray or not? I've never missed a prayer! I studied them all; that was over thirty years ago, and I remember it as if it were today. That teacher didn't just help me with praying; she helped me with many other things in life. And what many people don't learn until they're old, and what they're going to learn now with my book, is that responsibility is always ours, each with their own. In my case, there was no point blaming so-and-so or so-and-so, because at the end of the day I was the one praying there.

So if, reading this book, you think that at the height of your 25 years, some project of yours doesn't work out because your father and mother don't support you, congratulations to those two, because they're right not to support you; you're getting life all wrong. That's why you can't think of anything else to start these principles with other than the realization that it's up to you, dammit!

While you complain and justify yourself, saying that you're not fulfilled in your life because of someone else's lack of support, who are you supporting right now? We've reached a point where we start to think that people, who already have their own problems and are in need of support, should be supporting us, thinking about us, focusing their lives on us, when in reality everyone else is fighting their own battle. So stop demanding support from others. It's nice if you do, but when you put the burden on others, it becomes too comfortable. "Oh, I didn't work out because of so-and-so, so-and-so or so-and-so."

Another important point is in the professional sphere. "Gee, Charles, I've been working for ten years in the same company and I don't get promoted, my bosses don't appreciate me!" Then I say: "Man, your bosses are right! What are you doing differently? Are you studying? Are you arriving earlier and leaving later? Are you trying to learn new things? Suggesting solutions or just "punching a card" every day? If you haven't progressed for ten years, it's your problem and that of your boss who hasn't fired you yet! I would have fired you already!

Where self-responsibility comes from

Self-responsibility is born in the process of awareness. That's why it can be done in the act of reading this principle, and my concern for people is because we often draw conclusions in life about something without having all the information we need to do so. I can understand someone who hasn't had contact with me, or another specialist, thinking that everything in their life is shit because of others. But from the moment they realize what I'm explaining here, they've been warned.

Take another look at this example. If I'm driving along a road and my car skids on a bend because there wasn't a sign indicating a dangerous bend, it's partly not my fault; but if there are signs and I skid, it's totally my fault. So, when I tell you that it's your responsibility from now on, I'm giving you that sign. If up until now you've been skidding for lack of guidance or a map to follow, fine, I understand. Now, if you're reading this book and, after these pages, you think that it's someone else's fault that you haven't achieved something and not yours, well, you haven't understood anything, go back and re-read it because the responsibility is yours alone, no one else's, understand?

That's right, I've just dropped this bomb in your lap, saying that it's all your fault, but it's also all your credit. I've come to you with this responsibility, but the great thing is that you're better off than most people at the moment, because comparatively speaking we can always find someone who's worse off, and the world has improved a lot in recent years. According to data recorded in Factfullness, in 1800, around 85% of the world's population lived in extreme poverty and had a low life expectancy. Today we live much better than the kings did a hundred years ago; just take a look at the history of sanitation, food and health in general.

Despite this dynamite banana that I've now put in your hand saying that it's your responsibility, the point is that the world is a much better place to live in today. So stop complaining about everything! Today there's a strong tendency to say "Gee, the world has never been so bad", "Wow, there's so much hunger and misery", but then I ask you: on what basis are people saying this? I'm saying that the world has never been better, but I'm basing it on figures. And when I say something like that, I also take away the possibility of the person blaming the world, because they can say "I know it's not my mother's or my father's responsibility, it's just that the world sucks too". No, it's not! Luckily for you, the world is better, and to see how this is possible, take a look at the following graph.

Extreme poverty rate from 1800 to today

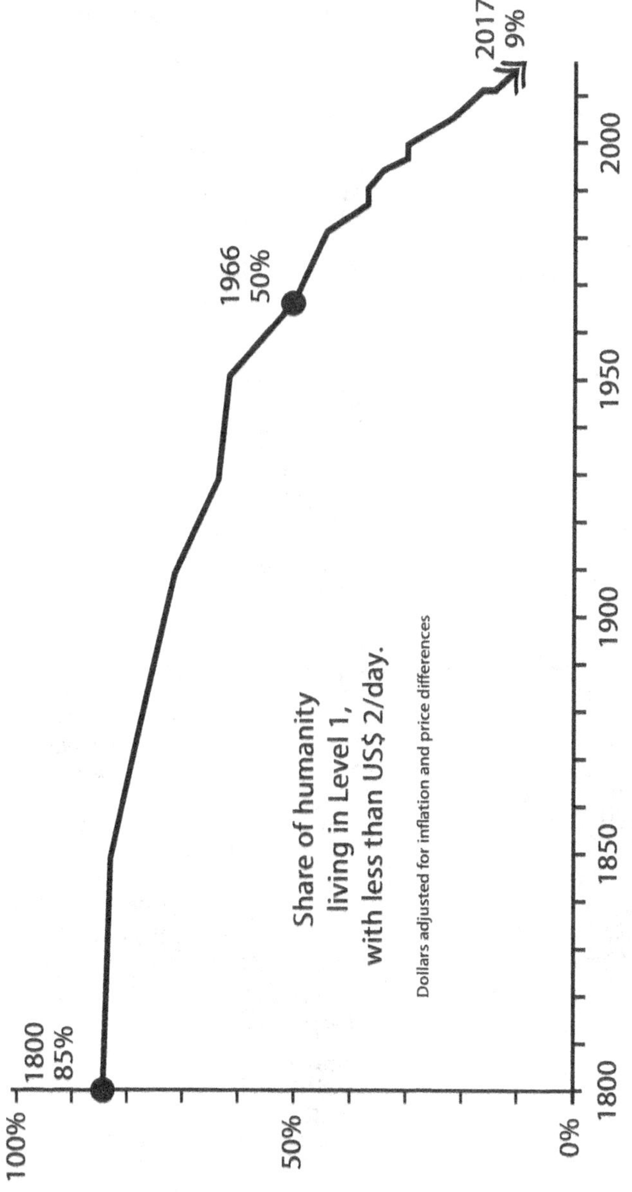

Source: Gapminder, based on Bourguignon and Morrisson, World Bank and OurWorldInData.

Principle

Follow your purpose

I've already told you here that I collapsed in 2013 because I wasn't living my purpose, but when I started following it, things happened for me. Now this doesn't mean that you should worry if you've been following your purpose for a week and nothing has changed for you. All I'm saying is that when we enter into our purpose, life starts to move and make sense, which is why, from the moment I started following mine, in a few years my life changed.

Following this principle may seem easy for those who have already found themselves in the world, but what about those who still feel lost? Come on, in order to locate yourself within your purpose, the first thing you have to understand is this: you are always the priority, and after that comes everything else, and what's important to make clear is that it has nothing to do with the ego. When we talk about purpose and you start following something, you have to ignore what's around you, because if you try to fit the world into your life, you'll end up messing it up. What do you mean? Simply put, you'll start thinking about everything you have and know at the moment, for example: "Gee, but I'm here in this place now, I have this job, this cost of living, this family, I have this house, this car, etc.". And if you start trying to shape your way of life and your purpose by what's happening in your life right now, you could be stuck in it for the rest of your days. So strip yourself of the world so you can think about your purpose.

I've also told you here that I talk to a lot of people, but the ones who are hardest to help are those who say: "Man, you just don't know, in my case it's complicated because I work, but I earn little, so I can't do this or that...". When people start saying that it's always much worse in their case, they're trying to justify a failure that's going to happen, and it's hard to talk to anyone in your life who hasn't had difficulties. This behavior ends up being a weapon for the person, who is shielding themselves from success. That's why there are people who don't give themselves any chance of succeeding in life. After all, they haven't even tried.

As well as having people who are difficult to help, there are those who are going crazy, and this has happened for two reasons: firstly, because most of them have no purpose, and secondly, there are a lot of guru's saying that we have to have a purpose. People who are lost in life, without a purpose, can't find themselves, they don't know what they're going to do, and nowadays everyone is shot by this information. In the end, the person even realizes that they have to have the blessed purpose, but where is the manual for achieving it?

You've always had a purpose

I could just say "here's my tip: find your purpose" and move on to the next chapter, but I'm not going to do that to you. First of all, my concern for you is divided into two: when you don't find your purpose, you're ruining your life and mine too. At that point I know you're going to ask: "But why am I ruining your life, Charles?". It's very simple: because everyone comes to Earth to fulfill something.

We have come to fulfill some mission. Forget my Jewish religion, forget your Christian or Umbanda religion, or whatever it is, forget it. Let's think in energetic terms. Everyone comes into the world to fulfill something in order to evolve, so if you come and don't evolve you're screwing up your life, the world, and consequently messing up my life too.

From now on, we're going to sort out everyone's lives here. Having said that you came here to fulfill a mission, let's go back in time. When we are born, we arrive knowing what our purpose is because it is basically a code that is in our DNA, a piece of software that has already been installed in our body. Therefore, our soul already knows what we came here to do with our lives, but sometimes it's us who get into fights with our purpose.

Do you want to see how you came with your purpose already in place? Pay attention to this question: when you were a child, what did you like to do? Go back in time and start thinking about it. When we grow up, we end up forgetting our mission, so it's as if we don't know it. However, we are already born with it, and the proof that it doesn't have to do with upbringing is the fact that, for example, we take two twins raised by the same father and mother, and one wants to be an astronaut and the other a footballer.

What habits did you have as a child? What were your hobbies? What kind of toys did you like to play with? At school, some people like history, others math, and there's even that crazy guy who likes physics. And each person liking a different thing is already a clue that the world is giving them about their purpose.

> If you're reading this 2nd principle and you've already found your purpose, great! Come with me and let's see if that's what it is. Now, if you haven't found it, we'll need to take a journey back, back to your childhood, rethink everything, bring back lost memories so that we can work on all this. From the moment you start making an effort to remember, you can make that journey back.

Another very important thing: stop thinking that purpose has to do with money. Don't think that if you're not going to become a billionaire it's not your purpose. When I say that everyone has a function here on Earth, you won't necessarily become a multi-millionaire with it, but by fulfilling your purpose, you'll feel very happy. For example, in a church, the priest is important, the pastor is important, but we can't take away the importance of the drummer in the band, the night watchman, because they are all fulfilling their purpose. A nanny, who throughout her life has been responsible for looking after and caring for several children while their parents are away at their respective jobs, is there anything more noble than that? Who said that someone who lived his life as an elevator attendant in an elevator had a mediocre life? If he lived happily within his purpose, doing it with love and care, he found himself in life, and lived fulfilled. He didn't dream of being someone else, because he was simply doing what he came to do in this world, and that's fine.

Everyone in the world has a role and a place. What am I best at? You can already do this reflection exercise, because the more we get to know the world, the more we get to know ourselves. Purpose is about happiness and prosperity, not money. Of course, to have a fulfilling life you'll need money, but that doesn't mean it has to do with millions, and many people are unhappy precisely because they ignore their purpose for the sake of money.

When we disconnect from our purpose, we end up going wrong somewhere along the way. Do you know where I went wrong? In 1993, I had my Bar Mitzvah. With the money I won at the party, I asked my mother to buy me a computer, so from that time on I was already very different from the other young people who asked for video games or a trip. I was that kid who played Monopoly. In 1994, I won the school World Cup lottery, and the prize was US$100. And what did I do with that money? I bought a modem! There was no internet in Brazil in 1994, but there was a thing called a BBS (bulletin board system) - it was basically that screen with a black background and a series of codes in green letters - and what happened? You could connect your computer to the other one, which was a great thing, and I built a BBS in my house that people at school could connect to between midnight and six o'clock in the morning, one computer at a time, with my computer at home.

When we go back in time and look at my history, what was it that I liked in general? Computing, computers, technology. I followed this growth, and when the internet arrived in Brazil I was one of the first to have e-mail, and I learned how to make HTML pages and everything. But when I took the entrance exam, I took it for computer science and economics, and the second option made more sense to me because doing computer science I could only work with that, and doing economics I could work with both specialties. And it was from this choice that for a good part of my life I tangentially focused on my purpose, because when I started working and entered the financial market, I needed to make money, and I didn't give a damn about technology. Over the years I dedicated my personal life to technology, but not my professional life. I wrote it off, so I was in the financial market, at Coca-Cola, I did various other things, and during this whole process, every now and then I would take a few risks, creating something on the internet, a blog, releasing a video on YouTube, but I didn't really dedicate myself to it, I never embraced it to live fully happily. It took me almost thirty years to understand all of this, because it was in 2014 that I really went online to live my purpose.

When I say to people: "Look, you're not in your purpose, you've been out of it for a long time", I say that because I myself ignored mine for a long time. Just look at how many people out there are depressed when they're not doing what they really came to do in this world. That's why it's essential to look back to the beginning of your story and understand what you've really enjoyed doing since you were a child.

Being on purpose doesn't mean that your life will be easy, but it will certainly be much more meaningful.

3

Principle

Define what you want in order to draw your map

For many people, winning in life means having money and a good job. However, I think that having a nice family is also winning in life. In terms of financial prosperity, it's having money, a good job or both. Now, it may be that the concept of winning in life for you is different, and that's fine, but what's the same for everyone is that in order to achieve a goal you need to know where you're going.

Anything that's too difficult, we try, try, try, until the brain realizes that it's not going to happen and makes us give up. This happens, for example, when you're drowning, or when you're running away from an animal that's running faster than you. There comes a time when you realize it's not going to happen, you give up and lose. So, based on this realization, what's the best way to achieve your goals without dying on the beach? Simply by drawing up a plan and sticking to it.

Whether your goals are financial, work or life-related, make a plan, no matter how big or small. In my case, I made a big plan to walk the 800 kilometers of the Camino de Santiago de Compostela. Obviously, I didn't get there by doing all 800 kilometers in one go, but I set myself the goal: "Today I'm going to do 15 kilometers". I didn't know if I was going to be able to complete the 800 kilometers, but I knew I could definitely achieve my goal of 15 kilometers that day. So I met that target. The next day, it was no longer eight hundred kilometers, but 785 kilometers that separated me from my final goal, and when I looked at the map, I soon found out how much I had to cover that day to reach my daily goal. How much do I have to do today? Twenty-three. Damn, that's possible!" I said to myself, already celebrating the success of my plan.

As I reached each stretch set as a goal for the day, I began to realize that reaching the 800 kilometers was possible, because that's how we let our brains and bodies know what's going on and, chemically, it makes a difference, giving us even more motivation to carry out the task we've set ourselves.

Having small goals to achieve a bigger one is much easier than always thinking about that goal and not being able to achieve it. So, for example, the guy who earns R$1.5 thousand and is thinking of earning R$15 thousand tends to get very frustrated when he receives a raise of only 20%, instead of being happy, which is more than all his friends are getting now. So not being aware of small goals and objectives sometimes makes you frustrated even at times when you should be happy.

"Ah, nice, Charles, but how do you organize all this in practice?" Very simple, you just need to be clear in your mind what your goal is, because it depends a lot on how it's configured. For example, we can even divide it into two: finance and work, which is my area of expertise. If it's work, you have to think: "What do I want for the next five, ten, fifteen years?". Dude, I know you're probably thinking right now: "Fuck, really? I've heard that before!", but that's the way to go. So, imagine you're an engineer and your goal is to become a director of a construction company. How do you get there? To become a director, you first have to be a full engineer, then an engineering manager, then another three hierarchical levels within the area, and so on, until the opportunity to become a director finally arises. You have to think this way, because when you're promoted from one position to another, you'll be happy with every achievement and you won't look at your director with that bad feeling, nurtured by ego, thinking that you haven't got there yet, while the guy earns much more than you. Forget that! What's your next goal? It's much easier to achieve something that's close at hand than to dream about something that's not going to happen, or that's going to take a long time. That's true in professional terms.

When it comes to finances, it's scary how many people fail to enjoy the journey. They need to learn that when you get to the end of a big goal, sometimes it's no fun at all. All the fun and beauty has been lost along the way and suddenly you haven't enjoyed anything you've experienced to get to where you are. If you want to have R$1 million invested - which is far above the reality of Brazilians - and you only have R$1 thousand, you'll get frustrated if you only think about how far you have to go to R$1 million. When they reach R$5,000, they won't even celebrate. Don't do that! You have to celebrate every step! Because when you reach a million, it's over, you've got there. You'll want five, ten, fifteen, we're all like that. I know people who have a good job, a good salary, good assets and no financial happiness, because they simply can't understand that they're doing just fine at that moment, at the present checkpoint. According to the Talmud, "a rich man is one who is satisfied with what he has".

We can imagine life as a big board game, so let's think about how to get to the next square. You need to move the pieces to each square. Sometimes, life gives us a little help and we move five squares at a time. That's great! But if you've only moved one square, that's okay, because the point is to move forward.

If you've made it this far in this reading, you know that whatever you're going to do, it has to be linked in some way to your purpose. And in this third principle, which basically consists of drawing your map, you need to organize yourself to establish what your goals are, and it doesn't matter whether you write them down on a piece of paper, on the wall of your house or tattooed on your back. Set goals towards the objectives you want to achieve, and then review everything.

Imagine the following situation: you join the company as a trainee and want to become a manager one day. To do this, you'll need to set some checkpoints, such as the time taken for each stage. How long does it take on average for a person to be promoted in the company? About three years from coordinator to manager? And you've been there for how many years? "I've been there for six... and my boss is shit!" Dude, I'm sorry to say it, but in reality you're the one who's screwing up, because you've already passed the average time, so you won't be promoted anymore. Once you've passed the average time, you need to look around for other opportunities, because it's much easier to control the average promotion period in your career than it is to dream about staying where you are. This is a very common characteristic of the younger generation. A guy comes in as a trainee and thinks he's capable of being CEO of the company. Things take time to mature. That's why you need to create a list of checkpoints for your brain, as this will help you to achieve the small goals that will lead you along the map you've drawn up for your objective. We can do this in different areas of life.

Careers

- Short-term: obtain a relevant professional certification.
- Medium-term: getting a promotion or moving to a more rewarding job or one with greater potential.
- Long-term: becoming a leader in my field or starting my own business.

Education

- Short term: finish the online course I've started.
- Medium-term: obtaining a university degree, postgraduate diploma or master's degree.
- Long-term: continuing to learn and develop new skills (continuing education).

Health

Short-term: establish a regular exercise routine, it can be as basic as one or two days, for example.
Medium-term: lose X kilos or reach a certain level of fitness.
Long-term: maintaining a healthy lifestyle and good physical condition, always remembering to eat a balanced diet.

Finance

Short-term: saving a certain amount of money or paying off a debt.
Medium term: invest in something (a house, shares, FIIs, a business).
Long-term: having a comfortable retirement (public and private).

It is always important that your goals are SMART - Specific, Measurable, Attainable, Relevant and Time-bound.

I give my own life as an example. I lost thirty kilos, but it was little by little, about two or three kilos a month for over a year, and I was happy with every kilo I lost. Now there are people who fight the scales for ten or even fifteen years and oscillate between extremes, hitting ninety kilos and wanting to reach seventy, saying they'll lose ten kilos in a month. Then, when they see that they've only lost three kilos, they get frustrated and go on to put on weight because they haven't reached their ten kilo target. That same person has never lost even five kilos, so why not put on two kilos a month so that at the end of a year they look wonderful? It just doesn't happen because people either want to do nothing or do everything and that's bullshit. There's no way to follow this all-or-nothing approach, because you have to do a little bit every day, and consistently, to get real results.

A lot of people come to talk to me about social media, because they know that my YouTube channel has grown a lot and so on. And they say to me: "I'm starting a channel too, I'm going to make a series of ten sensational videos, what do you think?". "Forget it", that's what I say. You don't have to post ten good videos on YouTube, you have to post two a week and keep it up consistently for a year. People insist on wanting to do a lot of things all of a sudden, then they give up and inevitably end up failing. The really good thing is to do things the right way for a long time, and that goes for everything in life. So much so that when you look at other areas that have nothing to do with work or money, it works, because we end up setting small goals in a very clear direction, to avoid wasting time, which is our most important asset.

Wasting time is a problem, whether professionally or financially. That's why it's very important at this point that you stop reading for a moment and reflect on the various areas of your life (family, money, work, studies) and ask yourself: "Am I clear about what I want?". Pay attention, if you don't have this clarity, you could be going in the wrong direction, and correcting the course afterwards is very difficult.

And when everything goes wrong?

In 2008, I was in Santa Catarina and had a great job as a superintendent at a finance company. At the beginning of the year, the economy was still hot, so I was getting a lot of job offers. I wanted to work for a big company, and some started looking for me. Headhunters were calling me and so on... I felt that, after ten years working in the same company, even though I had a good position and a good salary, it was important for my experience to suddenly make the leap to something big, in a multinational. "The time has come!" I thought.

Around July, I resigned, left with a good amount of money earned in the financial market and went to South Africa for a month-long exchange program to improve my English. I returned in mid-August, which was when the crash began, the crisis of 2008. Everyone was being laid off, a sea of people were being sent away. When I returned calls from headhunters, the answer was: "Forget it, nobody's hiring anymore".

I had done a lot of planning and had spent the last ten years growing professionally; so when I decided it was time to take a bigger leap into a larger company and grow further, becoming a director or even CEO, I found myself unemployed. I went from a scenario at the beginning of the year where I was earning a lot of money, with a super-stable and comfortable situation, with offers every month, to the status of an unemployed person who sent out CVs that nobody returned. It's a desperate situation, and I wasn't having money problems. But it's a business that affects your emotions, your self-esteem. Suddenly, from one moment to the next, I found myself at a loss.

You start sending out CVs, making phone calls, and people don't get back to you, they don't answer your calls. One day I got ready, printed out my CV, put it in an envelope and went to an executive recruitment and selection company in the South. It was still customary to contact them personally, but the attendant didn't even let me in, as she said I could send my CV by e-mail, and closed the door.

This is a terrible point for someone looking for a job: you send out lots of emails to the vacancies that come up, and often nobody replies or when they do, it's to arrange two or three interviews and you never get a call back. This is the anguish of the unemployed. One day goes by, two, three, and then you've sorted out everything you had to sort out at home and with the car, then the family starts: "So, when are you going back to work?"; friends keep asking you about work, you meet someone in the mall and the person keeps asking: "So, where are you working now?". Being unemployed" is a condition that shouldn't cause shame, but the truth is that only those who go through it know what it's like.

I was unemployed until almost the end of that year, when I got a new job in December. This bad situation lasted about three or four months, but it was shocking for me, who until recently had been living a reality of people pestering me to change jobs. But to this day I thank God that it all happened that way, because everything I went through helped me a lot to deflate my ego. Today I know what it's like to go through that experience, which I wouldn't have known if everything had worked out. I had to take a job to earn less than half of what I was earning before, in a much smaller position. I went from finance superintendent to commercial coordinator at Coca-Cola. That's what came up, and I thanked God when I got the job. I worked like crazy for two years and was promoted to manager, earning more than I did before. But now you calculate, from the moment I left my old job to achieving the status of earning the much-desired high salary was a process that jumped from two to 24 months to accomplish, because I had a major setback along the way, which was the crisis in 2008, so I had to retrace my route.

So, even if we do everything right, setting goals, objectives and everything else that's necessary, none of this is a guarantee that the map we've drawn up will work. Even so, you can't work with the "it's going to go wrong" hypothesis. Along the way, something is bound to go wrong, and we need to deal with that, but you can't stop having a journey and planning because you think it's going to go wrong!

You see, I had plans to work for a big company. A lot of things went wrong and suddenly everything was back on track. Now imagine if I'd given it all up? Moving forward sometimes creates a shock, an earthquake in our lives, but then things sort themselves out, which is why we need to persist in our purpose.

Fertile ground for prosperity

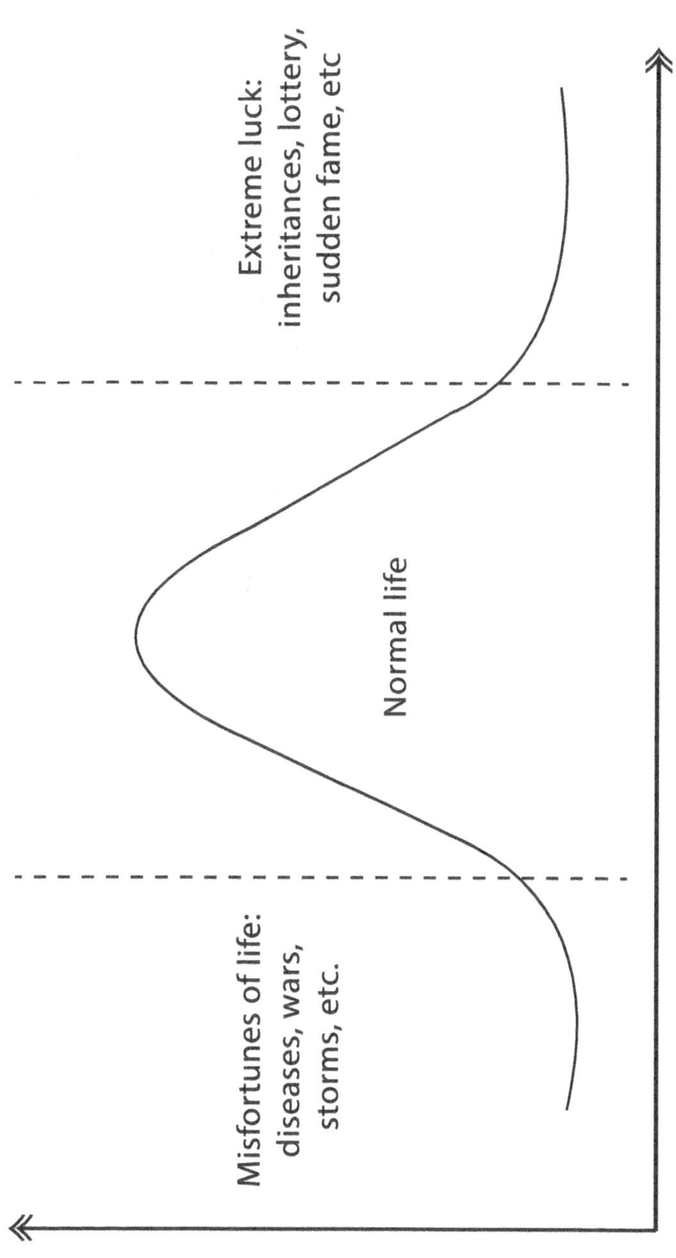

Source: Prepared by the author.

Looking at the graph above, we have people who go "wrong" in life because of very serious misfortunes, such as an illness, a storm, a crime, a bankruptcy. On the right are the people who do very well. The guy who wins the lottery, the soccer player who becomes a star, the person who marries someone very rich. Things they didn't even look for. It's possible that my speech doesn't fit into these extremes. However, for 90 to 95% of people, the reality I'm proposing is believable. And there will be people who say: "Oh, your talk is very nice, but I lost everything in an earthquake". I understand, I really do understand that everything fell apart, but you have to move on now. And there will also be someone whose life has been impacted by an inheritance and now everything is easier. At the extremes, therefore, there will be cases of exceptional ease or difficulty, but we can't take them as a rule.

I always say on social media that the "exception is the example of the idiot". Taking these rare cases and, for example, justifying that people don't need to study because Silvio Santos didn't study and is a billionaire, is a real crock of shit. Statistically, those who study earn much more than those who don't, so I prefer to work with the statistics that reveal what actually leads people to success, rather than focusing on these rare exceptions. A while back there was a video circulating on the internet in which an American boy told his father that he wasn't going to study, since Mark Zuckerberg hadn't finished school and still owned Facebook. The father then retorts by saying that Mark had entered Harvard before abandoning his studies... So, when his son first passed Harvard, they could resume the conversation.

The contemporary world is full of people selling ease. My speech isn't very pretty compared to what people are selling. I'm not saying that you don't need to study and that you just need to work smart and things will work out. I don't really believe that. I believe in small goals, work and objectives. Also, having a path is extremely important, and as long as you don't find it, you're screwed. "Ah, Charles, but what if the person has nothing in mind, doesn't know what they're going to do with their life?" Then "screw you!", I'll answer. But, you see, I don't think that not knowing what to do is a bad thing. Anyone who doesn't know what to do isn't 100% lost, they just need to find their way, so we're back to the story of purpose, childhood and everything else I mentioned at the beginning.

To draw the map, see the path of your purpose

Living with myself on the Camino de Santiago de Compostela made me see what I needed, and then showed me that I did certain things that I liked and that were already linked to my past, such as economics, technology and social networks. If at the beginning of my life my dream was to own a computer, and I loved playing Monopoly with money, what could be clearer than what my purpose was?

The path forces you to delve deeply into your self. If you take the long way, the whole French way, which takes around thirty days or more, on the first day you think about your family, about yourself, your wife, your parents. On the second day, something about work, a little problem you've had, and as the days go by, and as you get exhausted, walking alone in a forest or an open field, as all this happens, you reach deep areas in your physical and emotional aspect that are practically impossible to access in your day-to-day life in the city, in the comfort of your home, or with someone talking in your ear, or you giving someone a hard time, or still connected to the internet or wanting to see what's on TV.

So when you walk alone for so many days, you end up opening drawers that you never knew existed. I'm there alone, injured, with a nail falling off, a blister bleeding, the muscle no longer responding, then hunger, thirst, and you have to walk another fifteen kilometers uphill to get to the next shelter. This physical fatigue also makes you tap into part of your emotional state, it makes you question what you did to get there. In this situation, you have no choice but to keep going, every day you have to walk 15 to 30 kilometers, and you learn something very interesting:

The only thing you can't do is stop walking. You have to walk, because that's how things happen.

The similarity this sentence brings to life is enormous, because every day you have to get up and walk, take another step because that's how things happen. The Way of Saint James is a micro-ecosystem of life that we have. And I'm not saying that you have to go on a pilgrimage to draw your map, but that you will have to make new moves in your life, such as defining your objectives, preferably in writing (remember the tattoo?), and drawing up a plan of goals to achieve them, starting from the establishment of your purpose, to finally start moving the pieces on the board game of your life.

Principle

Ask and you shall receive:
the rule of intelligent projection

This 4th principle will only work if you first believe that it will work, and not the other way around, which would be to first see that something has worked and then believe it. Unfortunately, the concept contained in this principle has been greatly trivialized in recent years, especially after the media explosion about the Law of Attraction. Many people have started to create and sell products based on it, but the core of this thinking actually works. After all, how can anything work if you don't even believe in it? There's that cliché that "will becomes thought, and thought becomes action", and then you'll achieve your goal.

This premise sold a lot of products and became a fad, many people took advantage of this wave and it messed with people's heads. So I really believe that the first step for things to work out is to believe. Otherwise, you have to think about why you don't believe. If it's not possible and I don't believe, then what is possible? Now, let's bring this into the practical field so we don't stay in theory. Suppose I'm a manager and I want to become a director in the company where I work. Is that possible? No, there's no such possibility in this company because it's a family business, the owner has eight children and if the director, who is one of the children, leaves, in reality another of the owner's children will take his place. In that case, there's no point in thinking positively because in practice you won't get that promotion. Then you'll be frustrated, because if it's an absolute truth, it's over, if you know that here I won't make it, there's no point.

If you have a thousand reais in your account, and you want to have a million reais invested next year, and you have a job where you earn R$5,000 a month, is having a million reais next year possible? Probably not. So there's no point in thinking positively about impossible things either. And that's what a lot of people think.

However, I do believe in this concept of the Law of Attraction which says: "Positive thoughts cause the Universe to conspire in our favor". I totally believe in this, and then it depends a lot on faith, creed, it's important to put that out there. Even Judaism believes this. This is also a principle of realization, but those who don't have any faith won't believe it. That's why it's important to have this concept, because if you're from a Jewish or Christian society, which are the concepts I know, talking to God and asking is at the root of our faith. But we're going to ask, and he's going to set certain conditions without telling us. "Look, if you do all this right, it will happen". For example: I want to be promoted in my company, so I go there and ask God: "I want to be promoted, I want to be promoted...". Fine. Friday comes and what happens? I don't go to work, because there's a soccer match on and I make myself sick. Dude, in one of these situations you probably won't get promoted because you're lying to your boss, who may never find out, but God has a way of seeing what you're doing. So "ask and you shall receive" is actually "ask and you shall receive, but I'm making it happen".

"Oh, but, Charles, now I have to believe in God to get what I want?". You see, even if you don't believe in a God, faith itself is a scientific question. So how do you apply a question of faith to people who don't believe in anything? Simple. They can have faith in themselves, faith in the market. This concept of believing is perfectly applicable to a society like ours, where the majority profess the Judeo-Christian faith. It makes perfect sense. You talk to God, you express what you want. You commit to working for it and behaving in a way that is consistent with certain standards. Therefore, you will succeed.

But projecting a better future and asking for it can be very helpful even for those who don't have faith. The mere act of envisioning this future, for example, "I want to have so much money", or "I want to get to such and such a place professionally", or even "I want to have so many children..." allows us to put into practice the process we saw at the beginning, which is to set small goals, to achieve objectives. Doing something. Ask and you shall receive" may come to nothing if you don't believe in it. But why wouldn't you do something that has a good chance of working out and won't do you any harm?

Those who don't have any faith in this, in which asking is no use, and projecting into your future is no use, may not work in terms of faith, the concept of which is to believe that a greater force will help... But projecting a better future and asking for something, especially projecting a better future, will help you even if you don't have faith. Because by projecting that future, that place you want to get to, you'll be able to do all that project from the last principle, which is to set small goals, which is to achieve objectives, which is to do something. Asking to receive may come to nothing if you believe in it, but it won't harm you.

I think it's very important for people to have a notebook, something to bring ideas from the psychological plane to the physical plane. This is a process that needs to happen every day, whether it's writing or even vocalizing. What do you want? "I want to be promoted!". Then say it to the mirror, write it down, put it out there. It makes all the difference. Then you might even ask me: "NLP, Charles?". Yes! NLP in full vein! In 2018, I took part in an NLP program. I have a mentor in this area, and I can safely say that it made a big difference to me.

At the time, I was already recording videos for YouTube, and in August or so, the mentor asked me what my goal was. "I want to have a video seen by a million people," I said. In October it happened, and I was a long way from that goal.

I understand the importance of asking, of talking. It's a message to the brain. "I want to be a manager". Then I keep repeating it. One fine day, the director makes a fool of me, I start hearing rumors about my dismissal, I try to recover, I'm depressed, weakened... But the brain keeps the goal alive, because it's been reminded of it all along. It listened when I left. At some point, you convince yourself of what you need to do.

The same goes for a financial goal. You have R$10,000 saved and you want to have ten times as much. Write it down, express it. When the temptation arises to spend the money, your brain will question you much more than usual. "Damn it, didn't you want to save, didn't you want to achieve a goal? You've said it over and over again!" Then it's as if you've gathered an army of people to help you.

What I'm proposing here may seem obvious, but for most people it's not. It's good to talk about it, especially for those who don't have any faith, because it can be very helpful. This dynamic promotes a chemical change in the brain, in the organism as a whole. Accomplishing small goals gives you a great sense of pleasure, which is an incentive to face the obstacles that lie ahead.

Of course, you can't think you can achieve a goal by writing about it every three months, because that's a clear message to the world and to yourself that it's not important. Life lasts 120 years and you get discouraged because you've only tried something for a few months and it hasn't worked! That's why you need to ask for as long as it takes to get what you want.

When the book The Secret was launched in Brazil, the Law of Attraction boomed here. But the problem with this kind of movement is that people began to think that all they had to do was stay at home thinking positively and asking for it, and limit themselves to that. It's almost like wanting to have Schwarzenegger's six-pack belly by eating bread, drinking wine and skipping the gym every day.

You can have all the tools at your disposal, but if you don't act the way you have to, it won't work. Usually, a McDonald's works, but any franchise analyst will explain that among the units that don't work out, it's usually because the owner doesn't follow the guidelines. It's like a cake. From a recipe, I arrive at a result. There's no point in throwing in three eggs because I like eggs, or hardly adding any sugar because I don't like it... I can even improvise here and there, but if I don't at least respect the essence, everything tends to go wrong.

People waste a lot of time rejecting what works. If you have the tools, if you're receiving the tools provided in this book, if you're explaining everything beautifully, why run the risk of making mistakes? This is where that question comes in: is every Jew rich? No. I know many poor Jews. But every Jew, at least, has always been guaranteed to learn to read and write. Nowadays, everyone is literate, but five hundred years ago everything was very different. Since Jews historically have to learn to read and write for their Bar Mitzvah, celebrated at the age of thirteen, this has made them very different from other peoples. This cultural characteristic in itself changes the dynamics of the brain a great deal, and is one of the factors that help us understand the financial and professional success of the Jewish people. Study, work and faith.

Many people ask me about the Law of Attraction. For Judaism, it works. When I turned to mentoring and the neurolinguistic programming process, I already had a certain knowledge base about the Law of Attraction, but I turned to NLP because there is no end to knowledge. Even if I'm here writing about a certain topic, I'll continue to learn about it for the rest of my life. I like NLP, I like personal development events... And even when I'm in a place where I come across things I don't agree with or even don't like, I think it's valid, because I'm learning something.

What impresses me about being an influencer, as I said in an interview with Folha de S.Paulo, is meeting people. There are people who have cried while telling me how I've transformed their lives. I try not to cry, but I get emotional.

From a survey of my audience, I discovered that more than 60% of them are CLT or civil servants, 75% of them male. That's interesting, because many gurus and influencers are very hard on you if you're a civil servant. "That's a sucker thing." I don't think like that anymore. I'm talking to an audience that nobody is talking to. You don't want to be an entrepreneur? Fine! Get your company off the ground, invest more than others, and then you'll get a dividend on your investments, just as if you had a company. And nobody's talking to this guy!

5

Principle

Don't be mediocre,
do everything with excellence

I agree with the expression that "doing is better than not doing", but just doing for the sake of doing is not enough. You have to try to improve everything you do every day. You might even question this, saying that trying to do something, even if it's not excellent right away, is better than nothing, and you're right about that, because we really have to get out of somewhere and start doing.

The problem is that many people also do something mediocre just to say "I did it", without understanding that, over time, the more we do something, the more we improve, whether at work, in our investments or with our family. An example of this is my YouTube channel. I started recording videos in this format in 2017, and today, when I watch my videos, it's pitiful... I don't know how anyone watched them - maybe that's why so few people did! The audio was bad, the image was bad, I put on background music that you couldn't hear what I was saying... It was horrible. However, doing that allowed me to learn more about the subject, because I did my research and tried to improve.

When I completed between two and three hundred videos, I finally started to improve. And if you ask me if I made videos every day until I reached all that, the answer is no; some weeks I made five, the other week I didn't make any, the other week I made three, which was stupid, because I wasn't practicing consistency in order to grow my channel. So stop thinking that just doing is important, because it's not. Are you going to do a business? Are you already spending time? Then do it well. Do as much as you can.

Another very good point, contained in the book The Only Thing, is the Theory of 10,000 hours, which is very important for a person's development.

In 2008, Canadian journalist Malcolm Gladwell wrote the book Out of Series. His thesis was condensed into the expression "The 10,000 hour rule". In short: it's not natural talent that matters, practice makes perfect.

The origin of the rule goes back to a 1993 study carried out by Anders

Ericsson, a Swedish psychologist. He investigated the development of exceptional skills in professional musicians and concluded that those who reached the highest level of mastery had accumulated, on average, around ten thousand hours of deliberate practice.

However, it is important to note that the 10,000 hour rule is not a rigid, universally applicable formula for becoming an expert in any field. Although deliberate practice is an important factor in developing skills, other factors such as innate talent, opportunities, proper instruction and motivation also play a crucial role.

On my YouTube channel, I have over a thousand videos of various formats and lengths. Considering this period since 2017, I must have already reached these ten thousand hours, but I can still improve on this mark.

How can you aim for perfection if you don't work for it? We can work on two pillars: doing and improving the way we do it, looking for techniques, looking for all kinds of information to help improve what you already do. In my case, as well as recording for YouTube, I've done a lot of courses, training, attended events and watched countless videos as a form of laboratory. I still study and improve my technique today.

"Ah, Charles, but how am I going to do it if I don't know?" The answer is simple: as long as you don't know, you also have to do it, because just the act of finding out how to do what you want already takes you out of mediocrity and promotes an evolution in your growth.

So focus on these two pillars:

1. Do.
2. Do as much as you can, looking for tools to improve.

Before we move on to this topic of mediocrity, I need to make it clear that I mean "mediocre" as a synonym for "average". According to the dictionary definition, this word comes from the Latin mediocris, which means:

1. Which is in the middle or between two extremes, equals median;
2. Not outstanding in quality, value or originality;
3. Below average or acceptable.

In this way, if the average person does something and has an average result, you can even achieve a similar result if you do the same as them, and sometimes you can even accomplish something. If you are given a task at work and you do it, if you are mediocre, not in the pejorative sense, but in the sense of "being average", your result in the medium and long term will be average. If most people reach a number, whether at work, in their studies or in any other area of life, and they don't fall, but they don't advance either, they are average; and if you continue to be mediocre, you will have that same average result.

Okay, now how do we get out of this inertia? By doing things that other people - on average - don't do. It's not enough to do, you have to go beyond mediocrity. But you have to be careful with the common sense attributed to this word, so as not to give the wrong idea.

Normally, people tend to do what needs to be done without worrying about the bigger picture. But then comes the question: How to do it?

Rather than telling people what to do, we have to tell them how, otherwise we won't help at all. But back to the answer, it's very simple:

Do it many times and find the right technique.

If it wasn't already clear, I'd like to reinforce an important point in this book: we don't like exceptions here. The story that you know a guy who made it big on the internet by recording one or two videos is not the rule, because the reality is that you can't be a good influencer without recording a lot of videos, or a good footballer without training a lot, or a good swimmer without swimming a lot.

Many people tell me that they tried to get started on YouTube and it didn't work, but when I ask them how long they tried, they usually reply that they didn't persist for even three months. Dude, three months is nothing! To become a doctor you need to spend ten years studying. People are too fast, they want quick results. We underestimate the long term and overestimate the short term. We've swapped doing a little bit every day for "short-termism". "Oh, I'm going to record ten videos this week and make a splash on YouTube!" No! You have to record two hundred videos over three years, then you'll blow up. You don't have to go to the gym seven days a week for a single week, but go three or four times a week for the next two years. That's what brings much greater results.

How I got out of my own mediocrity

I'm very fond of a television program called Accumulators, which shows real cases of people who suffer from an obsessive compulsive disorder that causes them to stockpile thousands of things at home without ever getting rid of anything. And just like these hoarders, the average person also has this problem of carrying around things they no longer need. Sometimes the person earns well, is well off, but is accumulating a lot of garbage in their life.

Remember when I told you about my experience on the Camino de Santiago de Compostela? Along the way, I learned to let go of things that no longer served me and take only the essentials with me. And I'm not just talking about the material aspect, because as I began to clear away the debris in the field of my thoughts, I began to have new spaces to make new discoveries in the following years of 2014 and 2015. Just imagine, I was thinking of applying for a job at the same time as I was trying to set up a business. I didn't want to go back to the financial or drinks market. I wanted to move forward. So I opened a small transport company with just one truck, two trailers and a driver.

Despite all my enthusiasm, it was a very bad time because everything was too bureaucratic. It's hard to be an entrepreneur in some niches when you're small, and that bothered me and took me away from my purpose, after all I'm not a bureaucracy guy.

When 2016 arrived, I decided to kill the carrier and ended up in Silicon Valley, where I stayed for a month, taking part in an initiative called Mission to Silicon Valley with the people from StartSe, which is an educational platform focused on business. As I was already starting out with digital pages and my wine blog was taking off, I embarked on this venture. The mission only lasted a week, but I stayed for a month, spending the rest of the time trying to understand the Silicon Valley ecosystem.

This experience definitely brought me out of mediocrity, because I started making moves that I hadn't made before. I already had money, but instead of just staying in nice hotels in San Francisco, I stayed in the same Airbnb room as the programmers, to exchange ideas and understand how it all worked.

After thirty days, I came back, closed everything I had physically, which was the transport company, and began to devote myself entirely to online. The mission was like a confirmation of what I had imagined. Before, I was thinking of opening a wine store, a bakery, something physical, but I decided to stick to digital. Although there was always the fear of that famous question: "But is that all you do? Don't you have your own business?".

On the digital side, I changed the name of my news site from Smee News to Squad News. The following year, 2017, I opened my YouTube channel, and this whole digital turnaround began in 2013, with my wine blog, and came to fruition in 2017, when it became a fully-fledged business and my main business. It's been years, even though it seems like yesterday.

Over these five years I've also experienced various conflicts: Do I start a business? Do I take a competitive exam? Do I go back to the job market? But if there was one main factor that helped me out of my hesitation, I can say that it was time, because as time went by, I kept doing and feeling things. And associated with the time factor, I would highlight the question of purpose. In Principle 2, in which I talk about Purpose, I shared that mine was linked to the economy and digital, two universes that crossed paths in 2017, at the end of this period of searching and learning.

Since then, I've been doing the same thing. Although I created Economista Sincero in 2016, I only nourished it in its format in 2018. In 2017, I started 59 Segundos on YouTube as a response to something that really bothered me. On YouTube, the length of the videos gave me agony. I'd open a video with a topic I was interested in and, when I went to watch it, it was over an hour of someone talking about how they were going to their mother-in-law's place, how good their mother-in-law's food was, whatever. Why weren't people more objective on that platform?

Tired of this lack of practicality, I created the 59 Seconds channel at the beginning of 2017. The idea was to talk about everything, drones, wine, investments and even my own life, but in an objective way, "without beating about the bush", hence the motto of my channel, which remains the same to this day. I started recording on a variety of subjects, from how to open a bottle of wine, to removing salt from cod, to passing a coffee and flying a drone. But it didn't work, and I didn't understand why.

My videos were two to three minutes long, objective and I thought they would be a success. It took me months to find out why: YouTube didn't want you to solve people's lives in two or three minutes. The platform wanted videos longer than eight minutes, because then it could insert two or three advertisements in the middle of the content being shown. The longer the video, the more advertising guaranteed. So when someone searches for "Where to invest?" and there's my two-minute video and another 25-minute video, YouTube hides mine to show the longer one. I spent months making videos for almost nobody because of a mistake I made.

However, in May 2017, Bitcoin went up, so I studied the topic. I thought it was phenomenal, I invested and recorded a video for this channel, which had more views than all the others, and that caught my attention.

Look at my two purposes: teaching and social networking. From then on, my business was doing very well, but it was taking up a lot of my time, and I had to stop recording videos for YouTube because it was still a hobby and it wasn't working out.

However, at the end of that same year, cryptocurrencies began to boom; it was a crazy boom, and I started recording videos just on this subject. That's when the channel became 59 Seconds Cryptocurrencies. For almost the whole of 2018, I recorded videos just for this channel. It was a great laboratory, because that was the year I learned that I had to be frequent, it wasn't enough to be short.

I've had the great experience of having ten, a hundred, a thousand people watch a video of mine. Today, it's more important for me to have gone through all that and enjoyed the process than to have a single video with a million views. I've learned new things along the way.

When October 2018 arrived, the elections came along, and I wanted to talk about politics and investments, but I didn't think it was fair to cover these subjects on a crypto content channel. So I decided to upload videos about elections to the hitherto unknown Economista Sincero, which was born in this format.

It took me two years to reach seven thousand subscribers to 59 Segundos and, in February 2019, Economista Sincero already had much more than that. It exploded and overtook the other one to such an extent that I had to close 59

Segundos. I still tried to reconcile the two for about six months, but it got to the point where I couldn't do it anymore.

In 2019, Economista Sincero grew a little. But in 2020, already during the pandemic, I reached one hundred thousand subscribers on YouTube. In 2023, I exceeded seven hundred thousand, with an average of one hundred thousand views per video, and more than two million followers across my main networks.

After everything I've brought you in this principle, I'd like to ask you one thing: stop procrastinating and chase your dreams! Put your plans on paper, outline your objectives, divide them into micro-goals, execute them and go from day to day evolving, improving and don't stop, okay? Having a prosperous life is your responsibility!

6

Principle

Reading will take you further (and faster)

There are already eight billion people in the world, but only 46.8 million of them are rich. And do you know what all these people have in common? A very inexpensive habit that you can start doing now, and that there is a real possibility will help you a lot: reading.

So why not? If I were saying something like "every millionaire has a jet", you might think that you'd only have a better chance of being a millionaire if you also had a jet. That's fine, but then you'd have to have five million to make a habit of owning a jet. But no, I'm saying that, based on studies, millionaires read a lot, and many of them say that certain books have had a huge impact on their lives. So what's the point of not putting it into your life as a way of boosting your chance of success? I really don't see any reason not to read.

You see, if the billionaires themselves say that the habit of reading makes a total difference to their lives, why wouldn't someone read? What's more, this habit is probably the cheapest of all the possible options to maintain throughout life, and the one that can have the greatest impact on people's lives.

Bill Gates, who is one of the richest people in the world and has a great success story, reads fifty books a year, according to figures published in a recent article. Mark Zuckerberg, who founded Facebook and also owns Instagram, took the plunge into reading in 2015 and now reads a book every two weeks. Oprah Winfrey, the American presenter and one of the richest and most powerful women in the world, selects a book every month to discuss with her staff in her book club. Elon Musk, currently the richest man in the world, when asked how he learned to build rockets, replied: "I read books". What's more, if you want to talk about money, Warren Buffett, who is known as the best investor in the world, has said that reading is the key to success.

In addition to the fact that successful people share a common habit of reading, another point that stands out is that we are talking about successful people from different walks of life, different colors, different creeds and different countries. This means that the practice of reading is democratic and can be adapted to anyone as long as they want to read and see real value in this habit. The fact is, millionaires read.

For God's sake, people. What will be your excuse for not adopting the habit of reading books in your life after this?

Another important point, in addition to this discovery about the reading habits of millionaires, is that you increase your exposure to luck by reading, which increases your chances of prospering. And it's unlikely that in a lifetime, which we can consider to be up to 120 years, you'll be able to live as many stories as you'll be able to live these experiences by reading books.

I myself, for example, even though I've been traveling almost all the time throughout my life, I have no way of understanding, here in Brazil, what life is like in China, what life is like in India, what life was like in the Middle Ages in Europe. Obviously, I didn't experience it. But by reading period books, biographies and other similar genres, I can gain a greater understanding of the world.

"Gee, Charlão, I already watch movies about all the subjects in the books," you might say, and I know that movies are interesting, and I watch a lot of them too. But the wealth of detail in the books is usually much more interesting than in the movies. So reading The Lord of the Rings is much more interesting than just watching the movie. Both are beautiful. Now, there are a number of films based on books, both fictional and true stories, in which the books are infinitely better than the films, because they manage to bring out dialogues, subtleties, details and other peculiar experiences in the writing that the director of the film has to condense into an hour and a half!

Okay, I know you can watch the movie, find the summary on the internet or do anything else to find out what the book is about, but in this Principle 6 I'm going to prove to you why the habit of reading should never be ignored. And if you're still reading this book and haven't abandoned it after reading all the principles, let's move on to the practice part, which I'll divide into four categories.

Category 1: Those who have never read a book

If this is the case for you, congratulations! My book is your first. Or you may know people like this, who suddenly bought my book because they follow me but have never read it, so if mine is your first book in either case, congratulations to all of you, after all, you've come out of inertia.

Now, do you know what you have to do? Set yourself a very small goal from now on, for example, one book every six months. Look for content that will interest you as much as possible. Subjects that you like. Don't pick up big books. Then, little by little, you'll get into the habit. But be careful! You can't go, for example, six months without reading a single page. If you've come this far and bought my book, choose one more to read over the next six months.

Seriously, don't do this to yourself and go six months without reading a page. I'm asking you for one page. If you're reading one page, you've already taken the next step. Not reading at least one page for that long is practically an aggression you're doing to yourself, because there's no way you can't take a book to the bathroom, for example.

Think about it, in those six months that you haven't read anything, haven't you liked a photo on Instagram? Didn't you send a little message to someone on Facebook? Didn't you laugh at a little dance on TikTok? So, is it worth reading a page every six months at least?

Category 2: Those who read one book a year

If you've read practically nothing in recent years, congratulations, you're reading my book now! Try to see it as the first step in a change you're making in one area of your life, which is the intellectual area.

Pay attention, if I've just proved to you that reading is a habit of millionaires, by not reading anything, you're reducing your chances of becoming a millionaire. It's as if you were sabotaging yourself a little bit every day. So what I have to propose here is this: if you've read practically nothing in recent years, while you're reading my book, I even suggest that you do so now when you've finished this chapter, select the next book.

It's exactly like doubling your goal! If you already manage to read one book a year, you've already done the hardest part, which is to actually read it. Pick up a book, carry it up and down with you, start reading, get halfway through it and finally finish it. You know what you're doing. But what's missing here? Rhythm. Rhythm is missing and it's not hard to get it. So, for those people who get stuck on just one book a year, I propose a challenge, which is so achievable that it's possible to do a lot more, because I'm giving you a break that I don't usually give. If you're only reading one book a year, let's choose two for this year and three for next year, which means that over the next two years, you'll read five books.

However, since I'm giving you a hard time here, I want to ask you something now: you're going to choose and actually buy these five books. So I suggest you choose easy books. If you start a book and don't like it, please stop and replace it with another. Because people who read very little don't yet know how to choose the best books. They read so little that they start reading a book thinking they have to read the whole thing. I used to be exactly like that... Nowadays, if I start reading a book and I don't like it or I don't think it's good, I stop and give it a chance.

It's like I'm talking to a boring person, and if there's another nice person next to me who wants to talk to me too, what am I going to do? It's like the book is a person. For those who read a lot like me, the book becomes a companion. Anyone who reads one book a year should double their target. Because if we read two books in the first year and then double that amount, it will be four, meaning that at the end of two years we will have read six books. It's extremely possible, and for me it's a piece of cake. But I'm giving you this easy out because I want to squeeze you from the other side, in other words, I'm demanding that you buy these books, even if it's split up, three now and three later, because it's very important that in the next few days you buy... Or don't you want to be a millionaire?

In 2022 I confess that I read very little. I ended the year with twelve books read, which represents a bad year for me in terms of reading, because it was a year of changes, works... But realize that even so it's not such a bad amount, after all it's still more than the average reading in Brazil.

Category 3: Those who read three books a year

For those of you who have read three books a year in recent years, which is an average of one book every four months, I have a message: congratulations, because you are above average. Brazilians read an average of five books a year, with only 2.4 incomplete and 2.5 finished. So congratulations! You're already above average! That's the good news, but the bad news is that you're still close to average. In other words, you can get away with very little. Are you up for it? Great! So what can you do from now on? If you already manage to read three books a year, to increase that number, what's probably missing is a little organization, attention and discipline. In this case, you need to take a few precautions, such as putting your phone on airplane mode while you read, closing your computer screen, setting aside a day and a time for reading and not allowing yourself to go a month without opening a book, because often you may have read three books on vacation, but over the course of the year you don't read anything and then you feel sorry that you could have read more.

People who often never seem to finish reading need to improve their productivity. So if you've gone from the first to the last day of the month without opening a book, sound the alarm. You don't need to finish a book in a month, the problem is not reading anything, because then you're missing out on the opportunity to improve a little every month. Or are you still that student at school who leaves everything to study on the last day of the exam?

Before you tell me that you don't have time to read anything, I'm sorry to inform you: the lives of these billionaires, who sometimes run entire empires, are much busier than ours, but they are still organized enough to have time to read. "Oh, Charles, but I'm on the run..." Dude, Warren Buffet, who is a partner in several companies, a super-investor, with thousands of employees, etc., manages to read, and why wouldn't you? Priority!

Category 4: Those who read five books a year

If you're one of those people who read at least five books a year, congratulations! You're well above average. And before you think "great, can I cut it down to four then?", I want to remind you that multimillionaires started at this point and evolved, some to one or two books a month. But don't despair, you're already on your way. The next step is to reflect on your reading. Are those five books you're reading a year helping you in various areas of your life? Are you making the best choices? From now on, just as important as increasing the quantity of books, since you've created this habit, is increasing the quality in parallel with this quantity.

You've already done the hardest part: you've created a habit that most Brazilians don't have. And not only have you created a habit, you've also managed to maintain it. That's why it's also important to always seek out the best reading for ourselves as we read more and more. How? By searching for topics, reading books on areas that interest you, but also new areas that can open up your horizons, you can try to include biographies or even historical books, if you're not already reading them. We always have to look for reading that adds to us, we have to improve the value, as if it were the added value of our reading. For example, imagine you read five books a year, very good books. In five years you'll have read 25 books, and if they're good books, they could completely change your life. Now, you might be thinking: "Oh, I'm reading five books a year, but only books like Harry Potter, Lord of the Rings...". That's why I tell you, one reading is better than none, but we can always improve.

"OK, Charles, but why didn't you say in the other steps what I should read?". Very simple, because first you need to create the habit. If you got into the habit of reading with Lord of the Rings, that's fine with me. But there will come a time when you need to get out of it and look for more challenging reading. It's as if someone came up to me and said: "Well, I'm starting to drink, I drink beer". Then I say: "Yes, that's fine, now I'll teach you how to drink wine". The point is always to improve. That's the highlight of this principle.

Finally, whenever you are discouraged by your situation, remember that Solomon preferred knowledge to money. Therefore, the more knowledge we acquire, the greater our chances of changing our lives. I can say this because, as well as understanding in theory how this dynamic works, I have also experienced it in practice. Don't think you'll get far without knowledge.

Principle

Pursue knowledge every day

Solomon was the richest man in the world, king of Israel from 971 to 931 BC, and his wisdom is still the subject of study today. So, in order to bring what we can learn from Solomon into practice and the modern world, we need to pursue knowledge on a daily basis. However, many people, especially at the beginning of life, give up knowledge at work, of being in some way close to people who have a great deal of knowledge in exchange for money.

So sometimes people don't want to be trainees at a company, they prefer to work elsewhere because they'll earn a bit more and they don't want to work with someone intelligent when, in reality, especially at the start of life, the more knowledge we can acquire from people who have real knowledge, especially in the practice of things, the more we'll be able to advance. For example, I worked with several people who had a lot of knowledge. I felt that this was happening and I stopped going to places where I could earn more because I wanted to continue working with people who knew a lot, even if I earned less.

So, as well as understanding this principle in theory, I've also experienced it in practice, because the more knowledge you acquire, the further you get. And don't think that if you're getting very far without knowledge, you won't somehow pay a price for it later, because if you're getting far without knowledge, that means you could actually be getting much further. That's the fact.

So pursue knowledge on a daily basis, even more so since I talked about books in the previous principle. You can pursue knowledge in many ways today because information is free, decentralized, and you can get it through YouTube, Instagram and other social networks and online platforms.

Now, for example, from the Middle Ages until the 1990s, how could you acquire knowledge? By reading and knowing someone who had knowledge, that was the chance. So someone who lived in a city in the interior of Brazil would often have difficulty accessing the knowledge of the guy who lived in New York. There was a separation where geography itself played against most people; if I lived in the interior of São Paulo, for me to have the knowledge of the guy who lived in New York about some things, I would have to move to New York, I would have to have money, I would have to have a series of conditions. However, with the advent of the internet in the late 1990s, the game changed.

Today we have all the information we need at our fingertips, whether we pay or not. Is paying cool? Yes, and do you know why people pay for knowledge when it's free? Because normally when you pay, you pay to have a trail, you pay to have a path, you pay to have a facility, but free knowledge is already available.

In the 1990s I started studying English, until my family couldn't afford for me to continue. So I stopped due to lack of money. Then, when I started working at the beginning of the 2000s, I started taking English again, but as I worked all day and studied at night, I began to struggle. I couldn't go to English classes because I worked so much. Do you know what happened? I had to stop taking English classes because there wasn't a course near my house or near work; I couldn't organize my schedule because I had to physically go somewhere, I had to travel half an hour to get there and back, not to mention that one day it rains, the next day the sun is shining, so one day you can't go, the next day you get mugged... it's horrible!

So how does it work these days? Anyone can open YouTube, type in "how to learn English" and millions of options will appear - while writing this principle I decided to do this test and 327 million results were found. Can you see how everything has changed? You can't learn English today if you don't want to. What's the principle? Pursue knowledge every day. Then you have to see what you need to know and start pursuing it now.

If life used to be a race with barriers, many have been removed in recent years, and geography is one of the most difficult. How could you learn certain things living in places where you didn't have that knowledge? It wasn't possible, you had to leave. Today, anyone in any municipality in Brazil has access, with a computer and the internet, to any kind of knowledge free of charge.

I remember trying to study English on Saturdays in the center of Rio. It was expensive, I had to go in person, so I started working every Saturday and Sunday. I tried to go at one time or another, paid for a year, and still couldn't make it. You know that roll? That's what I had at the time. But today I can sit comfortably in my living room, any day and any time, and study whatever I need for free. So there are no excuses and no waiting around!

⁂

Nowadays, it's much easier to access knowledge, especially with a cell phone in the palm of your hand. First of all, it's important to know that the more we seek knowledge in a given area, the more we thrive in it. That's why it's very important to always seek to learn on a daily basis, because it's building this habit that will propel you even further.

But as mentioned earlier, many barriers have been removed in recent years and decades. So it's become much simpler not only to consult subjects of interest to us, but also to follow people of interest on our social networks. I know that new media can be an escape when we want to distract ourselves, but social media can also be a tool for learning more and more, daily and free of charge. And now I ask you: "Well, if you're a programmer, a lawyer, are you actively following people in your field on social media?".

It's also important to follow these people who generate and create digital content, not only because they sell it, but also because much of what they transmit is already available for free; they are capturing leads, in other words, they are attracting this audience by creating valuable content that enables them to acquire knowledge in various areas.

In Principle 7, you have to make an effort to expose yourself to luck, and what does that mean? To explain, here's an example from the story of Bill Gates, which became famous because of the book The Psychology of Finance. Bill Gates went to a high school in Seattle with three hundred other kids in 1968. This school was one of the only ones in the world that had a computer, because some guy in the community thought it was important to have one. Everyone shrugged at the computer, because it didn't have a function yet. It was the 1960s, but even so, one guy thought it was interesting, held a bazaar and bought a computer for this school in Seattle where these three hundred kids were studying. At that time, the chance of a child having contact with a computer in the world was less than one in a million, and Bill Gates went to this school where he had access to a computer. He and Paul Allen, the other founder of Microsoft, went there.

They were both interested in this new technology at the time and began to like it and take an interest in it. Today, Bill Gates says: "If it hadn't been for that computer, there might not have been a Microsoft".

So what happened? In this case, he was exposed to luck, it was a fluke, but he was there. Did having contact with computers guarantee the future of all the children? No, otherwise we'd have three hundred billionaires, which is how many children studied there. The presence of a computer at school didn't guarantee success for everyone, but he himself says that it was essential for his company.

So what conclusion can we draw from this? The more you are exposed to "luck" and the more you seek knowledge, the greater your chances of prospering. You may be asking yourself: "Oh, so I'm only interested in luck?". More or less, because there's also the other side, the risk side, in other words, bad luck.

In this story about Bill Gates, there is a third friend of theirs, called Kent Evans, but this third friend was mountaineering and ended up dying. The chance of someone dying mountaineering at that age is also less than one in a million, but the guy exposed himself to the risk anyway. What lessons can we learn from this? You have to expose yourself to knowledge, look for ways to improve, evolve and try to avoid risk at all costs.

There's no way of knowing the exact figures, because there's no research into luck or risk... but we can think of it like this: most of the population leads an average life. We wake up, we work, we study... But there is a portion of the population that is unlucky. And what does that mean? Unfortunately, a car accident, a plane crashing, a company going bust... sometimes it's your fault, sometimes it's not, and you didn't do anything wrong... So I have a friend who, unfortunately, his parents were in a car accident, the guy was orphaned and lost all his money, screwed up in life, at the beginning of it. But that's not his fault.

On the other hand, there are people who have the famous "ass facing the moon". That person who's really lucky, the guy who wins the lottery. It's the person who suddenly marries someone very rich, and it's not a scam, the person really did marry someone very rich. It's luck, that person who got lucky and everything worked out in life. She went to work for a company, the company went public and she made a hundred million... I know people like that, who didn't have any money, went to work and it worked out. This has happened in the United States with some startups where the guy was just a service provider at Facebook when he started, he did some wiring, and then Facebook didn't have the money to pay him, so they paid him in shares at a ridiculous price and then he made millions...

So it's luck. "Oh, but the guy took it, he was a visionary...", fuck no, he took it because he wanted the job. So there are the two extremes, but there are also the people who are here, who are living... For example, if you're unlucky, imagine the person who worked all his life at Banco Nacional, which went bankrupt, like Banco Santos, or the guy who worked for one of Eike Batista's, put all his money in the company and lost everything... so that's the unlucky person, the average person and the lucky person.

But what's the big deal? We've already realized that we have to try to expose ourselves to luck, it's possible to try, you know how? By getting close to intelligent people, trying to work in good places, reading more, improving your life... If Bill Gates had contact with computers and evolved, damn it, if I have children, I'm going to try to get them into a better school, into music class... I'm going to try to expose my child and myself to things that make us evolve.

What's the big problem I've noticed talking to people? Normally those who are here have a view of the world that that's all it is, or that the world is luck, or even that the world is a lack of it. The problem is that, for a large part of the population, it's not that they're unlucky, but there's the guy who was born in a poor country, who lives in a community, who doesn't even have much access to water, health or education. It is precisely this person who finds it difficult to understand that they can evolve.

While we have Bill Gates at one end, we also have your friend at the other. That's why I say: you can be in many different situations throughout your life, but the important thing is to always try to evolve and improve your current condition.

That said, be prepared for luck. It happens a lot in my field, social media, that people say: "Hey, Charles, do you know that guy? I've seen you in a photo with him, all of a sudden this guy exploded on social media, he's grown, he's evolved...", then I reply: "The 'all of a sudden' was ten years of the guy working".

The principle is: the more you are exposed to knowledge, the more this luck can happen. Luck is also related to preparation, which in turn is related to knowledge. You might say: "Well, cool, everything you're saying is interesting, but the theme here is to pursue knowledge on a daily basis". That's true, but what I'm trying to convey is that chasing knowledge on a daily basis will mean that, if a job comes up, you'll have "the knowledge"; if a business comes up, you'll have "the knowledge"; if you meet an interesting, single person and they're interested... The bigger this bubble of knowledge, the greater your chances of prospering in everything, in relationships, in jobs, in relation to money... That's the north of Chasing Knowledge. Otherwise, if you're not going to improve your life, why pursue knowledge? For vanity? For ego? It doesn't make sense.

In addition to pursuing knowledge on a daily basis, this search for knowledge should be done in a targeted way, correlated to your area of activity and also to generic knowledge, because those who keep their knowledge strictly to their area of activity can end up "narrow-minded". When you study other areas of activity, you expand your horizons.

I worked in the financial market and then went to work in the drinks market, and in that market there were a lot of people who only knew the drinks market, so I was often able to innovate because I had other knowledge. And there, I also understood that knowledge from other areas can often help you in your field.

8

Principle

Adopt mentors, even if they don't know you exist

We've already mentioned in the book that, after the end of the 1990s, with the advent of the internet, geographical barriers fell and knowledge spread to all parts of the world. As a result, we put an end to one of the major problems that limited people's evolution, which was contact with mentors. And these mentors can be spiritual, professional, gurus, you name it. In my mind, a mentor is someone who has reached places you haven't yet reached and want to reach. It's important to explain what a mentor is because I don't want you to think "I don't need a mentor, I'm fine here". The question is: do you want to evolve?" "I do", so fuck it, go and listen to someone who's already got to where you want to be. Because this guy can help you a lot on this journey, you don't have to make the mistakes he made and he's always warning you.

The importance of mentoring for you can be divided into two parts:

The first is to give the right direction. Because if someone has already got there, they know the way. It's like climbing a mountain, you don't have to look around every corner, finding out which rock you're going to cling to, the risk of falling... if you talk to someone who's been to the top, to the peak, countless times, they'll be able to show you the way. So the mentor's first point is to give you the way, to give you the map.

The second, which is just as important as getting there, is to get you up to speed, because you'll be able to get there on your own without a mentor, but you run the risk of falling by the wayside or taking much longer to get where you want to go and, probably, when you get where you want to go, you'll want to go somewhere else. So, it's like life is a video game in which we unlock new stages. The mentor can say to you: "Look, now there's a trap. Now get down. Now jump. Now get the key. Now be careful not to lose your life".

Now that you know what a mentor is, who will take you where you want to go and speed up the process, what can you do to adopt a mentor?

Well, the first part is that the mentor doesn't need to know you exist. Today, many mentors (entrepreneurs, scientists, influencers...) disseminate their content for free online. The first way you can connect is simply by hitting the follow button on their social networks. It's as simple as that. Have you solved your life in this area? Absolutely not, but you've already taken the first step. What would the next steps be? Reading biographies, as we talked about in Principle 6, reading will help you a lot in understanding other people's lives and the path they have followed.

So, you can follow people on social networks, you can read their biographies and, if you want to take longer steps, many of these influencers, gurus and mentors have their paid events, even in person.

Having said that, you can follow, evaluate and everything else, it would be very interesting for you to immediately look for people - again, I'm going to hit on this - who are related to your day-to-day affairs, but who also work in other areas. Which areas, for example? Health, obviously from reliable sources, people who have studied a certain subject. Today you have information that we didn't have twenty or thirty years ago. So all the information we know about health, about sugar, fat, soft drinks, healthy or unhealthy diets... is available, and there are still experts who speak to the general population on social media and who may arouse your interest in talking to your doctor, or looking into a particular subject in more depth. Following mentors in the health field can greatly improve your life, so the health field is already one of them.

Another area: spirituality and meditation. Meditation has been proven to enhance our mind.

Meditation and spirituality are areas where you're unlikely to get the best people in the world in your area, wherever you live, even if it's the best capital in the world, you won't have all the best experts living in one place, but they all live on the internet. So you have all this at your disposal.

All the world's great experts can be your mentors and gurus, even if they don't know it. Physical exercise, reading, development. Who are the experts in the areas in which you want to evolve? Do you know who they are? - "I don't know". Get on Google, do your research, jump in. Because when you really want something, you go for it. It's a question of making a decision, because once you've made up your mind, it's over, nothing's going to stop you, you're going to get it into your head and face anything.

You may be thinking: "Do I need mentors? I already have a degree, I have a good job...". Look, you may not need one, but Bill Gates did, Warren Buffett did and all the great billionaires and entrepreneurs did. So you can go a long way without mentors, but you'd certainly go even further with mentors, because if life - as I like to say - is one big puzzle, with lots of information, mentors can give you many more pieces than you could manage on your own.

Buffett had his mentor in the financial area, and he evolved a lot with that. But how long would it have taken him to learn without this support? Maybe he wouldn't be where he is today without a mentor.

Man has lived much longer without so much information than with all the information he has today, so you who are reading this book are probably from the first generation to have access to so much information and so many people for free. Take advantage of this because, in time, it will be so common for people to understand how to take advantage of this kind of availability of information that it will no longer be a differentiator. So take advantage of it, we're in the middle of a technological turning point, it's an opportunity, and those who know how to take advantage of it will stand out.

You're just in the process of evolving, because it's only once you've organized your life that you'll be able to make even greater leaps towards financial independence. After all, there's no such thing as financial independence if you don't get your house in order first.

I'd like to give you an example: luckily, in my life, I've managed to break down geographical barriers and have had contact with mentors physically. In the companies I worked for, especially at the start of my career, I had bosses to whom I owe a lot, because they demanded so much of me every day (and I hated them so much for it at the time), that I started to give more than the maximum I could do, and this led me to results I never expected to have. They pushed me in such a way that I evolved immensely.

I also had my grandfather (and my hero) in my family, who was my mentor because he never let me accept being a mediocre person. He also demanded results from me and I realize that this had a big impact on my life, because my grandfather was my mentor in business, money, spirituality, he was my guide to Judaism, and he awakened the curiosity I have today in the world. My grandfather, between the 1960s and 1980s, took the money he earned and traveled a lot with my grandmother, at a time when nobody traveled the world. So, when I was a child, one of the things we did was go to the airport when they traveled. I remember as a child picking up my grandfather at the airport when he returned from his trip around the world. And that's how he sparked the curiosity about the world that I have today.

And then you might think "Charlão was very lucky"; yes, I was very lucky, but you're ignoring the fact that there's always the other side of the story. My father abandoned my family at an early age, we had money problems, and my mother still had to rely on my grandparents to help me and my sister grow up. I could write a book about the difficulties in my life, but I'd much rather focus on what helped me get further. I'd rather try to evolve and not write a book about victimization.

As I talk to a lot of people, I often get counter-arguments like these:

- Oh, I don't have any money.

- Oh, I don't have time.

- Ah, I have bad luck with that.

- Oh, my father abandoned my family.

Man, one justifies oneself and doesn't focus. I can't help you change what happened in your life before this book, but I can encourage you to change from now on.

Understand something, you get out of where you are the moment you move; if you don't do anything different from your ordinary days, it's over.

Think about waking up earlier, reading a new book, researching new subjects, meeting cultured people, eating healthier, etc.

I, for example, walk for forty minutes on the treadmill, that's forty minutes of knowledge every day, because that's when I listen to a podcast, watch a video, take a class... forty minutes is a lot of time.

9

Principle

Exercise spirituality

In this beginning, I'm already going to propose that we differentiate between religion and spirituality so that you don't come back to me and say: "Oh, Charles, I liked the book, I'm enjoying everything, it was good up to this point, but I don't have a religion, so I'm going to skip this principle". If you do, it's because you're confusing religion with spirituality, so I'll start this principle by explaining the difference between the two.

Religion is a set of practices, customs, rituals, traditions, dogmas, beliefs that include a supreme external force that shows you a path to follow, that's a religion. We also have the question of penalties and bonuses along that path, so in religion you have principles, dogmas, things you have to follow, organizations, methods, timetables, food you can eat, food you can't eat, celibacy in some doctrines and in others not...

So in religion you have these customs, practices and traditions with penalties and bonuses along the way. And religion includes what? A Pope, a Rabbi, Jesus, Mohammed. One interesting thing about the religions that have moved the world for centuries is that with religion you are part of a group, it gives you a sense of belonging. So I take comfort in knowing that I'm not alone in the world as a Jew. In Brazil, for example, the evangelical movement ended up entering communities and being very important, because in my opinion it took the place of the state. People help each other, people understand each other, they make movements and organizations like the Sopão, they donate food baskets, clothes, toys, and so on, I consider this movement to be one of the best things that has happened in Brazil.

Now, religion has this problem of penalties, that is, if you eventually marry without fulfilling a ritual or sin in some way, there will be a penalty, but religion gives you this feeling of belonging, that is, it makes you feel part of a plan, which includes other like-minded people. So that's a religion.

Now, spirituality, which is the theme of this principle, can be summed up as believing in the good, in a higher energy, or not, and that it can be on your side on the same plane. It doesn't require rituals, beliefs or dogmas.

There is only the will to become a better human being, a person who judges others less, who charges less, who helps more, who tries to listen to others, who is sensitive to what is happening in the world. So, to be spiritual, you don't need to belong to any group or follow anything, you just have to try to be a better person every day. So we share all this.

I particularly like the combination of the two, religion and spirituality, because they can bring you hope; this has often helped me, and it also helps many people. When I did the Camino de Santiago de Compostela, I was looking for a bit of that too, to find myself, to understand what motivates people, to understand what's going on. But if you've come this far, you're enjoying the book and you don't believe in a religion, this principle is also for you, because spirituality is for anyone, since I've explained here that it's about believing in the good and wanting the good of others. Do you want these things? Then you're already at the beginning.

Many people have a certain resistance when we talk about spirituality, because they think you have to be religious to be spiritual and that's not the case; in fact, it's exactly the concept presented here.

Now, I'm going to share with you a story about hope, as well as religion and spirituality.

Once, the great wise Rabbi, Rabbi Israel Salanter (1810-1883), was spending the night at a shoemaker's house. Late at night, Salanter saw that the man was still working by the light of a flickering candle that was almost extinguished - in other words, he passed the shoemaker's house and saw that there was a light. The Rabbi approached him and said: "Sir, it's late, your candle will soon go out. Why are you still working at this hour?". Without being swayed by the Rabbi's words, the shoemaker replied: "As long as there's light, you can mend".[1]

1. *The Book of Jewish Values, a daily guide to ethical living*, p. 69.

So - we can put the whole story here - the story here is saying that as long as there is light, there is hope, so as long as we are alive, there is hope, and that is the principle of spirituality. In the story, the author talks about mending, in other words, it's the same as remedying a difficult situation, just as we can reconcile with those we've distanced ourselves from, help bring peace to the family, do charity, help a friend.

⁂

Spirituality can help us seek to do good and try to be a better person, regardless of your religion. So this point applies to everyone. It doesn't matter if you're Muslim, Jewish, Christian, Umbanda, it doesn't matter what religion you are. Here I'm talking about spirituality, about wanting the good of others. As long as we're alive, we can do good.

In short, the key to this principle is exercising spirituality. However, how can you think that exercising spirituality, for example, is reading the text, praying the rosary or, in my case, not eating forbidden meat and so on? If you're still confused about this, go back to the beginning of this principle and look at the difference between religion and spirituality.

⁂

Okay, having understood what spirituality is, how can you get from zero to something? By immediately doing what you can. I have nothing to do with anyone's life, I don't want to know where they are in life, but I do want to help.

If you've discovered that spirituality is about doing good, wanting the good of others and creating a better world, you have to look inwards and see: today are you a person who makes the world worse, the same or better? Which of these three areas do you fall into? Only you can make that judgment. "Well, Charles, in recent years I've become a resentful person because I'm not happy in my job", or "I'm not happy because my wife left me", or "I don't think the world has been fair to me". Well, cool, you're making the world worse because you think the world has hit you. So take advantage of this moment and reset it. The world has hurt you and you're giving it back to it, which consequently contributes to it becoming an even worse place. So, if we're talking about spirituality, about wanting to do good, you need to wipe the slate clean and start from now on... There's no point in dwelling on the shit you've lived through in the past.

Back to my case, for example, I've lost four children. Is there any point in me beating up the world? Do I dwell on it every day? Do I badmouth my friends who have children? Do I look down on people who have children? Or is it better to exercise my spirituality and understand that this must have happened for a reason and that the only thing I can do is try to act in a way that improves the world and that, at some point, I will understand what happened to me?

When we've just experienced a problem, we can't understand at the moment why it happened. We came into this world to live a life of 120 years or so, but the world itself is millions of years old, and so we rush around trying to understand everything? It's impossible! Therefore, the guy who has been hurt by the world in some way, and pays it back by hurting everyone, is not very reasonable.

Following a behavioral analysis of the various profiles of people and their relationship with spirituality, we have the case of a neutral person, who basically says: "I don't exercise my spirituality, so I don't owe anyone anything. I'm here in the world to get what's mine and I don't believe in any plan beyond life. This is it, this is life, we come from dust, we go back to dust and fuck it". You may be right, maybe you feel good about it, but would it hurt you too much, take up too much of your time or would it be so damaging if you tried, just for an experiment, to exercise your spirituality for a year?

Listen to someone a little more, don't speak badly of others, try to police yourself. As an experiment, I'm asking you here. Look, do you think it doesn't matter if the world is one way or the other? Okay, I can't prove to you that it makes a difference, can I? But what I can do is ask you, could you, extraordinarily, for one year, act differently? Just to see if your own life changes; now, if nothing happens, you can go back to being a selfish person, and mind your own business. Everything is going well for you, you have a great career, you have money, a happy family, you think it makes no difference to exercise spirituality, to want the good of others, and everything is fine. The only thing I ask of you here is that you try for a year, no more and no less, to take care of this aspect.

Now there's also that whole group of people who already exercise spirituality. "Charlão, on Sundays I serve soup to elderly people, I dedicate my time, I'm at a good point in my life; my wife and I get together once a month and donate clothes to someone..." Dude, cool, keep it up. Probably, throughout your life, as in mine, you're going to take some very big blows, and then the challenge is, while you're taking them, to keep exercising your spirituality, because while everything is fine I also know how to exercise my spirituality, but the moment you take a blow and fall to the ground, that's when I want to see you exercise your spirituality. Even though I'm not a resentful person, I understand that at some points in life, practically everyone goes through some situation in which they think the whole world is against you, as if it were a divine conspiracy, which makes you believe that you don't have to be a good person. Not to mention the number of people who do the wrong thing and see it work out. How many people who do wrong have money, power, status, fame. However, point number one is that we don't know the person's whole story and, secondly, we have no idea what the future holds for them, so looking at this kind of thing only makes us not exercise our spirituality.

10

Principle

Be generous and keep your account with the Universe up to date

We've already talked about religion, spirituality and being better people. But what if you ignore all that? Will it have any practical effect? I mean, if you decided not to follow spirituality, or be a better person, or improve who you are... in short, you didn't follow any of this, will there be any punishment? Perhaps not. But can't we try to imagine the world, the Universe, as an account where everything good you do leaves you with a positive balance?

If you start to think like that, isn't it worth starting to act in a certain way so that your balance is positive with the Universe? Many people call this process other things, for example, the "Law of Attraction". There are people who say that there is such a law, and that all you have to do is think positively for things to happen; all you have to do is do a good deed and something positive will automatically appear in your life. Man, it's impossible to say anything like that. There are even physics studies about this, and they even claim that cells act differently with positivity and with other things, but I still believe that man will need to study much more about all this.

In any case, it's interesting to think about keeping our current account with the Universe always positive. I love the story of a rabbi called Menachem Mendel Schneerson, who is the best-known rabbi of the last generation. Known as the Lubavitch Rebbe, he was a sage respected by Jews and non-Jews alike; born in 1902 in Ukraine, he ended up growing up in the communist era, as they ended up dominating the country after the 1917 Revolution, persecuting all religions, especially Judaism, banning services and executing their members. In 1928, he moved to Berlin, where he married and studied mathematics, philosophy and physics. With the rise of Nazism, he moved to Paris, where he graduated in mechanical and electrical engineering.

So realize that he is a rabbi, one of the best-known rabbis, if not the most famous in the world, but he studied various areas of science not related to religion or spirituality. In 1941, the Lubavitch Rebbe managed to escape before the Nazis took France and went to New York, where he led the local Jewish Community for decades.

Now the most curious thing about this rabbi's story is that on Sundays he would spend hours handing out one-dollar bills to thousands of people. So basically, on that day you would go to the synagogue, where a huge queue would form, and he would give you a blessing and a dollar bill, a blessing and a dollar bill. Thousands of people every Sunday, and he gave each one a dollar bill. And do you know what this was all about? Basically, the person who left with the dollar bill had to donate it to someone who needed it. So his purpose in the world was this: he gave you the dollar bill and you gave it to someone else, which in short means that when two people meet, a third person should benefit. If we always thought like that, the world would be a better place.

So, to have a positive account with the world is to think about the following: how can you benefit the world directly and indirectly based on what you've just read and the last principle so that your account in the Universe is positive? We don't know what will come next for the world, after all, each religion has its own point of view, but if you leave here with a positive account, you'll probably already be doing very well. What if the world is just here and we're buried and that's it, it's over, have you lost anything by being a better person? What was your loss?

What's also interesting is that the rabbi said that helping people is very worthwhile, even if you have to go out of your way to do it. It's an act of kindness that deserves our attention and effort. And then you might be thinking: "Okay, but I'm not a rabbi, I don't live in New York, I haven't suffered persecution all my life". Fine, but what about when you order food from the app delivery guy, do you get off before he arrives so the guy doesn't have to wait around? Do you tip him? When you order an app car and you know the driver is coming, do you wait at the door or do you sacrifice the other person's time?

Doing good and having a positive account with the Universe can be much easier than you think. Our small acts can make a total difference to someone else's day, but it's something active, you have to think about it and do it, because it won't happen all of a sudden.

So what you have to do now is stop and think, "Well, in my day-to-day life, what can I start to change now so that someone else can benefit?".

When we try to be a better person, we always have to be careful, because everything leaves a trail in the world, both for people who are close to us and who are not relatives, such as at work or in our community, and for our family, which will extend to our children and grandchildren.

I remember my grandfather, every time we went out for lunch, dinner or somewhere else, he would give a much higher than average tip. Way above average, in fact. He gave money to everyone. That really caught my attention and I'm a very similar person, so how much did that affect me? What if he was a greedy person? That's why we have to take into account that being a good person and helping others, as well as having the direct effect that you've helped that person, can reverberate in a way that you can't even imagine. So my grandfather may have made that gesture to help one person, but indirectly he helped hundreds of others because he set an example for me, and I follow that example and do the same now.

Now imagine if my grandfather had raised me and one day he had said to me when I was, I don't know, ten, twelve or fifteen years old: "Never tip anyone; people don't deserve it, and they already earn their wages". If he had said that, perhaps at that moment in the formation of my character it would have been this master record that I would have kept for my life: "People have their wages, they earn what is fair and they don't deserve any more". But no, no matter who it was, he always had a note of money, if it was R$100 he would give R$150, if the guy came to do I don't know what, he would give money, if the guy came to carry the suitcase, he would give money. I saw him doing this, so in my mind it's right that we always give a bit more money (to those who have it, of course).

I've kept this habit, but it could be different. What if everyone acted like that? "Oh, Charles, but maybe the other person doesn't deserve it". The thing is, we're not talking about the other person, we're talking about ourselves. That's the big question, it's not about the other person, it's about me. "Gee, Charles, but what if the guy takes the money and uses it to gamble or drink?" My action simply stops at the moment I donate the money, in other words, if I donate money without knowing that he's going to use it to drink, I'm not impacted by his bad action, because my good deed was done and ended at the moment of the donation. Don't use this as an excuse not to help people, like, "I don't know what they're going to do with the money". It's not up to you to know what they're going to do with the money. That has to make all the difference.

In Judaism, there are certain rules for helping someone, including rules on whether or not you can communicate that you've helped, so, for example, helping someone anonymously has more value within Judaism, within our rules, than helping someone and spreading the word to everyone. But even if you tell everyone, helping someone is quite an achievement, so it doesn't lose its value. Besides, in the act of helping someone, the highest priority of all is the hungry; any other help can be discussed once you know what the person is going to do, but the hungry have to be helped.

11

Principle

Improve a little every day

You're probably thinking: "OK, improve a little every day, but what do you want me to improve at? You want me to read books, eat better, treat my spouse better, start walking every day, take a course... I'll go crazy! You're going to drive me crazy, Charles!". Well, that's not what I want. I don't want you to improve in all areas because you must have already understood, or at least you will understand in this principle (and if you want to go deeper into this topic, I highly recommend the book Essentialism, by Greg McKeown), that you need to focus and make choices, because those who prioritize everything prioritize nothing.

When I say to improve a little every day, you have to know the following: "my priority, now that I'm 150 kilos, is to take care of my health"; "my priority, since I'm 35 and haven't finished high school, is to finish high school". In other words, it's you who will dictate which area of life you have to improve. I'm just here to tell you that every day you stop is one less day to do this, so you'll evolve less in the areas you want to. So what do you have to do now? Define, over the next few months, the main areas that you will commit to improving. And how many areas can I work on at the same time? Two or three at most.

It's possible to improve in all areas simply by dividing and evolving a little in each thing, but you have to focus on two or three areas that you want, and over the next few years develop more, whether it's your health, your technical training, your relationships, if you're a person with relationship problems... First, you have to define which area you're going to choose, because I can't decide for you. And if there are areas that you're already good at, just keep at it. If you're at a good weight, eat well, walk five kilometers every day, great! That's it! But what other areas do you also want to develop?

I can speak for myself too, as I once weighed almost 130 kilos. I went through several weight loss processes in which I would lose weight and put it back on again, and do you know what the mistake was that took me so long to realize? I wanted everything "yesterday". So, until 2013, every time I managed to lose weight it was by using medication and going on very strict diets, in other words, things that I was incapable of maintaining in my day-to-day life.

So when I say to improve a little every day, I mean not to rush the process, but also to do your best to finish it as quickly as possible. In my weight loss process, after trying crazy things several times, I managed to lose more than thirty kilos in about two years without any medication, just by changing habits, cutting out certain foods and doing a little exercise every day. That way, I didn't run, I didn't do anything special, I simply went to the gym every day and walked on the treadmill, after all, a person weighing 130 kilos can't go out running.

That's why I'm here setting an example, and I've tried several times to lose weight quickly, but I only succeeded for a short time and then I ended up failing again. Once I understood that it was a process of continuous evolution and that I had to stick to it, I succeeded. But beware! I'm asking you to improve a little more every day, but I'm not telling you to find a shortcut in these areas of life, because it's important to find a way of improving that you can maintain.

The story of how I managed to lose the weight is about the area that was the most sensitive in my life and, looking at all the areas I study, this was my biggest deficiency. It's important to understand that, normally, we're going to have some point that's a bit more fragile, including some people who have serious problems with binge eating and who, for example, when they resolve this issue, end up transferring the compulsion to the sexual or financial route, because all of this is connected.

So the first thing you have to do is control yourself, and if you can't do it on your own, seek help. I, for example, couldn't lose weight on my own, so what did I do? I went to a nutritionist, who has been with me for over ten years, and why? Because she knows my shape and understands, for example, that I like wine, so does a diet plan that doesn't include wine work for me? No, it doesn't. But in order to include wine, it's necessary to remove something else, to dose the amount I drink... In this way, we need to work within our reality, but without forgetting to improve a little in each area.

Another interesting point: when I say improve, it's not necessarily just health, or family and relationships. There are many fields you can think about evolving, for example, your certifications, studies, networking. "Well, work isn't that important to me, family is more important"; if you're thinking this, then you already know what you need to improve. However, at the same time, is it possible for you to put your work as the fifth, sixth or seventh item on your list of priorities and have an extraordinary result in your work and finances? It's not possible. So be careful, because if you want something extraordinary in any area of life, you need to make an extraordinary effort in that particular area.

"Well, Charles, I want to have a good career"; if I'm talking about improving a little every day, you have to organize yourself and plan ahead. Now, imagine that you are a CLT and have a career in a bank. What do you have to do in your planning? What certifications do my bosses have? What tips can they give you? Have you ever had lunch with someone above you to ask for information? Are you humble enough to seek out what you need to get where you want to go?

So, improving every day means that you have to select certain areas and really evolve in them, otherwise you'll only fool yourself, your family, your friends and the people you work with, and they know who you are. Since you're not fooling anyone, you have to evolve a little more every day.

I admire Bernardinho, from volleyball, who has a very interesting phrase: "Winning is a consequence of preparation", and he goes on to say that "the will to prepare has to be much greater than the will to win. Winning is a consequence". Great athletes prepare and have a passion for the process. I have a passion for the process of everything I do. In other words, improving a little every day means understanding the importance of the process of evolution and learning to enjoy it.

This also includes motivation and discipline. Nowadays, people talk a lot about motivation, there are even motivational events and everything is about motivation, "wake up, take a cold shower and you'll be motivated", when, in fact, motivation is a state of mind. In this way, you often don't need motivation. I work several days without motivation for one reason: discipline. It's this tool that made me lose thirty kilos, because when I opened the fridge and wanted something, I'd think: "No, I can't", and that's pure discipline.

You will only be able to evolve in these areas on a daily basis if you have discipline, so I ask you to stop reading this book and take out a pen and paper. Now write down the areas you want to improve immediately. I don't care what you do to make it happen or how you motivate yourself, because I'm concerned about your discipline. Are you closed?

You don't need motivation, you need discipline. "Well, I'm super motivated by reading the book", great! That way you'll have motivation and discipline, even better! However, what you need to improve every day is discipline, or do you think the guy who trains swimming is happy to jump into the freezing water in the morning in winter? Do you think he's motivated? He hates it, but he does it anyway because he has discipline. He loves the process because he knows it's important. And that's why this guy is a winner.

So it's about these areas of life that you're going to stop now and write about.

12

Principle

Be selective about who you hang out with

Show me your friends and I'll show you your future.

There's a lot of talk about "you're the average of the five people you hang out with the most" and because of this, it's become a cliché. However, no matter how many unsuccessful people repeat this idea, it's still true. When you talk to successful people to find out a bit more about their life path, it's almost unanimous that being close to them doesn't guarantee success in itself, but it does help a lot. There are reasons for this and that's what we're going to discuss in this principle, as well as showing you why you can change this in your life today.

In the past, as I've already mentioned in this book, life was more difficult because there was a geographical barrier. There were still physical distances, and the digital world has opened a portal that has changed everything. But what do I mean by that? Basically, if you were born in the 1970s or 1980s, in the countryside of a Brazilian city where there were no successful people around you, you would probably have to leave there to rise in any area you were interested in. However, after the 2000s, the scenario changed completely, and wherever you are it is possible to socialize, even if only digitally, with people at a different level. Even so, geography still matters a lot.

To help you understand this idea better, I'm going to give you some examples from my own life and that of people close to me. When I was out of my teens, I went to college and started working; I had lots of friends, with whom I played ball on the beach, and we went out all the time. But as soon as I started working I realized that, more at work than at college, there was a whole world inside the company I worked for, and the people who led me, or who were close to me, had a lot to add to my life.

So, in the first few months, I ended up distancing myself from my friends a bit, and why? Because it made more sense for me, on a Saturday, to be working, attending a meeting, going to a company event, studying a bit more... It made more sense than being around people who didn't have the same ideals and goals. It wasn't easy. I remember passing by on the Via Litorânea in Rio de Janeiro on my way to work on a Saturday at eight in the morning and seeing some friends going to the beach carrying a soccer ball or a surfboard. It may seem easy to say now that things have worked out for me, but I know the price I paid, I know what I gave up to get here.

So when you take this attitude, at whatever age you are, whether it's in your teens, at the end of your teens or even in adulthood, something will happen to you. What I've seen happen to many is that you don't have to abandon those people who don't add anything to you. In fact, you'll be purged from these groups. This happened to me and to several people I've met. I'll say it again: what you're reading in this book is the fruit of 25 years of work, study and a lot of professional and personal experience.

To be more specific about this issue of being purged, imagine that you live in São Paulo, start working and investing, but your closest group of friends get together every Saturday to have a barbecue and watch soccer, for example. It's only natural, and I'm telling you this will happen, that when you start investing in shares, real estate funds and everything else, at the first barbecue you'll want to talk about it. And what will happen next? You'll see that this isn't a topic that these people want to talk about, and not because they don't like money or don't want to improve their lives, but because they don't understand what you're talking about, so it becomes something very distant from their reality. You become the boring guy in the group.

At that point, two things will happen: firstly, you'll be upset because you started a topic that no one followed up on, and then, as soon as you turn your back, your friends will all say: "How has so-and-so changed, he's so boring, all he wants to talk about is money, all he wants to talk about is investment, it's like he makes so much money out there". These two situations will go hand in hand and you'll be purged from this group. On the other hand, and this is by the way a good thing, if you start studying, working and looking for digital or physical sites where people are seeking growth through knowledge of the same topics, you will make new friends who have the same goals - to prosper, to learn, to change jobs, to start their own business.

This Principle 12 can cause discomfort, just as it did for me. To this day, I consider some of my friends from my teenage years, I talk to them regardless of the distance, but the daily interaction for me and, above all, for them is no longer as interesting, because the topics are no longer the same. I like soccer, but in some face-to-face meetings, like lunch and so on, between talking about business and soccer, I much prefer to talk about business.

What's interesting is how people seem to remain static. We are in an evolutionary process, and if we dedicate ourselves a lot, work and study, we do change. But there are still many people who insist on having exactly the same mindset as fifteen, twenty, thirty years ago. The person still runs the risk of becoming uninteresting, because how are you going to talk to someone who has limited content? Then you might ask me: "Okay, I get it, now I have to be careful with my friendships; from now on I'll sort it out... Well, that's it, we're done with this topic, aren't we, Charles?", and I'll tell you right now that no, we're not done. In fact, we're just getting started.

The easiest thing is to resolve the issue of friendships, because you can easily lose touch with most of your friends, and in the end only those closest to you will remain. You can also make new friends very easily, either at the MBA or at a meeting, and, for example, if you want to make new friends in the investment world, go to meetings and investment fairs. In other words, you don't need a miracle or any great effort.

Now here comes the difficult part that not many people talk about, because they focus on the "little click" of the five friends and forget two important points: family and spouse. Here are the pitfalls, or the spring that can throw you over the edge. People only talk about their friends, but you come home every day to sleep with your wife or husband, and not with your friend!

So, starting with our family, we see the world from different perspectives of awareness and experience... However, we carry a lot of the lessons that our family has passed on to us, especially when it comes to money. Phrases like "money is dirty", "everyone who is rich has done something wrong", "it's hard to earn money", "we'll buy it back", are just some of the things that have been part of our upbringing and, in this way, everyone replicates this model in their lives. Our parents and grandparents always acted in a way that they often couldn't even explain to us why, but their parents acted like that, but it's up to us here, with conscience, to change this line of succession of decisions.

Getting rid of friends and groups is very simple, but how do you do it with family and spouses? Well, with regard to family, it's important to understand that you don't need their blessing for anything, you don't need their permission or approval, and you shouldn't take all criticism into consideration. The family is here for you to love and be loved, and if you stop some plans and projects because of your family's opinions, don't blame them, because you're the shit.

For you to understand better, I'll bring up my example again. My father abandoned my mother when I was still young, so I never knew him, and my mother raised me. Up until the moment I'm writing this book, she's never listened to a podcast or watched any of my videos, because every time I've sent them to her, my mother has said that the link hadn't arrived or that it wouldn't open... Interestingly, though, she's sent me a lot of other people's videos, but she's never seen mine. That said, have you ever seen me complaining something like: "I've stopped recording videos on YouTube because Mum can't see them"?

It's not possible for someone in their 20s, 25s or 30s to stop doing something because their parents, grandparents, uncles or cousins criticize or don't support them. Even without any heavy criticism, I've seen people give up their projects because their parents didn't support them. So fuck you if your parents don't support you, fuck you if your uncle criticizes your learning about investments, don't care if your cousins make you a laughing stock at the family barbecue because you're talking about how you want to own a car that no one has ever owned, how you want to travel to a country that no one in your family has ever visited. Ignore them.

Now, am I asking you to "not love your family and not hang out with them"? Never! What I'm saying is just the opposite. You will segregate these areas, hug your mother, your father, kiss everyone and be happy. If they don't care about your projects, your work, your financial life, fine, that's good, because in the end it's all about you. I'm sick of seeing people in their forties still blaming their parents for something in their lives. I think this is an excuse because they don't want to face up to their own responsibility.

So what you have to do is separate these two aspects, the personal affection part from the professional, financial and prosperity part. The sooner you separate the two, the better. The important thing is that you do it. With friends we do it in one way, taking care of them, having the same affection, but separating them. With family members it's different, because I don't recommend anyone separating from their family, unless it's something very destructive, but apart from that, if you know how to put each thing in its place, you'll do fine.

So far, so good, but then comes the part that I consider to be the most difficult: the spouse. This is the point that, with the life experience I've had and the conversations I have with many people and followers, is perhaps one of the most important variables, if not the most important, in a mathematical equation for success.

Who will you spend your life with? Who will be the person you spend every day of your life with? It's impossible not to think that this will make all the difference.

This is how we got away from the cliché of the "five people who sit at your table" to divide people into three types of relationships: friendship, family and love relationships. And this is important because no one has looked at the sphere of family and spouse, everyone just focuses on "who you're hanging out with"; but then the person comes home and has a toxic fucking family, or the person decides to get married to get out of the house and ends up in a relationship with someone completely outside the box.

Let's imagine that you're going to be married, God willing, for forty, fifty, sixty years to the same person, which means that the impact of your relationship and your cohabitation will weigh heavily. I'm not going to go into the specifics of relationships here, it's not my area of expertise. So I'm going to talk about the following: what are the impacts of being with a person who, when you buy a book, asks you: "Is this book going to make you rich? Wouldn't it be better if we spent that on a snack?". What are the impacts of being with a husband who, when you think about joining an investment course or going to a free seminar at the weekend, complains that you could be doing the dishes or the laundry?

What are the impacts of a crap relationship in the short, medium and long term? It's devastating. That's because we're talking about simple things, but there are much more complex issues, for example, how important it is and how much you think it can impact your life. If you stay with a person who, for the first two or three years in a new job, is going to support you in the extra effort you're going to make (and should make since you're in a new company), how much is that going to impact your life?

For example, I've always been a person who worked a lot, including weekends, and I've had relationships in which the person got in my way, demanded my presence and gave me a hard time, criticizing the fact that I wasn't available for the beach, cinemas and weekend programs common to any couple; and others in which the person helped me, pushed me forward and got on with her life, even doing a master's degree, while I worked weekends. Do you see the difference? She understood that this was important to me and began to occupy her time while I worked. Curiously, a few years later, that master's degree she did while I was working enabled her to have a job with very high earnings.

So, look how crazy and interesting it is that, by trying to occupy her time while I occupied mine, in a constructive way, she unknowingly guaranteed her own future by trying to guarantee mine. Now, let's imagine a scenario in which she kept honking in my ear: "Charles, do you have to work on Sunday? But it's Christmas Sunday. Your boss is already rich, stop being a dick". If she'd been nagging me all the time, would I have grown in the company or would neither of us have grown? I would probably have left the place where I became superintendent precisely because I worked harder than the others, and then she wouldn't have gotten a great job because you had to have a master's degree to hold that position. I supported her, she supported me and we both grew up. It's very easy to imagine that this scenario could have been totally different, we could have spent two or three years on the beach at the start of our relationship and then lamented that life is unfair, that meritocracy doesn't exist and that everyone who gets a good job is because they have an acquaintance in the company.

This is just one example, but we can think of many others. Both men and women who get married and just spend their own money, don't support each other and, worse still, make fun of people when they want to evolve; this is brutal, in fact, the ultimate level of destruction within a relationship.

Imagine you're someone who thinks for weeks that you want to study something new, but when you tell your partner, he or she laughs and says you're too old to learn it. It's hard enough to get on with your life without anyone criticizing you, but criticism, especially from people close to you, makes it much worse. Unlike your friends, you can't meet your spouse whenever you want; you have to meet them every day, so if you're with a negative person who pulls you down on a daily basis, there's no point in reading my book. That's because there will be no change in your life if you think about all these principles, spend hours reading them and, after closing the book, spend another fifty years with a person who speaks and acts in a completely different way.

With all this in mind, there are two ways out: dialog, through which you will settle this and come up with a common plan; or, unfortunately, what happens to many couples and is part of life, separation. But life doesn't end there; sometimes, on the contrary, it begins there.

You may be thinking: "Oh, Charlão, but I'm not dating yet, I'm not married". Good! Good, because that means you have a blank page, and it's much easier for you who are reading this before you get into a relationship than afterwards. You'll have signs throughout the relationship if you're involved with someone who mocks and diminishes your dreams, and if that person is someone who doesn't support you; you have to think carefully about the future of this relationship, because I guarantee that everything, for better or worse, will be amplified once you're married. That way, something that starts off small, that is a pebble in your shoe, if you don't remove it, will bother you for the rest of your life.

Last but not least, let's look specifically at the issue of values and money. I've seen a lot of couples who fall apart, who take bigger steps than their own legs, and a very common mistake is the anticipation of dreams. So, you want to invest, you want to have extra income and you're thinking about the future, but you've married a man or woman who wants to anticipate dreams. Anticipating dreams happens when you have a nice car, you get a raise, and your husband or wife says: "Gee, didn't we deserve another car? Don't we deserve that?", and so you go on spending, always anticipating everything, as we said before. You anticipate everything you want and you get into a rat race, and you never get out of it.

So be careful not to get involved with someone or spend years with someone who makes you live a life that only seems prosperous, because you might have everything you have, but in that situation you'll always be on the ropes, and no one on the ropes feels truly good. If you're living at a lower level than you could, you can live happily because you'll always be at ease.

Now that you've understood the point made in this principle about how damaging it can be to get close to the wrong people or to remain close to them, I want to reassure you. You have all the time in the world, so you can make these changes little by little. I'm not talking about cutting ties with your childhood best friend, who you meet once a month at a barbecue, and stop talking to him just because he's not interested in the same subjects, that's not it. What I'm saying is: divide your time so that most of it is focused on what you want for your future. And the same recommendation applies to your family and spouse.

13

Principle

Understand once and for all
that money is your friend

As we said in the last principle, we often carry beliefs, values and information about money that are not true or that we have acquired from family, friends and spouses. The most common belief is that money is dirty. Many people also have difficulties because of this. They have created this belief, so few people understand that money is your friend, that it is here to help you and that the world abounds in riches.

It seems a bit crazy to say this in a world where so many people are in need, but we need to try to look at the globe as a big table where a banquet is taking place, where there is "idle" money and you just need to understand the way to get to that table and get your hands on whatever food and money you want. It depends on how you act.

Now, what do I mean by "money is your friend"? I'll give you a practical example: let's imagine compound interest in relation to money, you can owe money, for example, on a credit card or overdraft, paying 100, 200, 300% interest, as is classic here in Brazil; or you can learn to save, invest and earn that money, not to the same extent, because investments pay less than debts, but you can earn that interest to your advantage. So, by understanding that money is your friend, if it's lacking now, it will soon be in abundance, and by understanding this logic, you remove a huge block.

In my life, in addition to the family experience through conversations with my grandfather, there was something that really impacted me, which was reading the book Rich Dad Poor Dad, but why? Because in this book the author portrays the difference between his contact with his own father, who was a spiteful teacher with great difficulty in dealing with money, even though he had a theoretically stable life, and his contact with the father of a friend of his, who was a serial entrepreneur and who had no problems with money because he treated money as a friend.

I had this double contact with my grandfather, who taught me this, and with the book Rich Dad Poor Dad, and perhaps the impact of the book is as great as that of my family, which also helps me to prove to you that the geographical barrier is no longer a problem today, as I said before. In other words, regardless of the city in which you're reading my book, you too can buy Robert T. Kiyosaki's book and have him as your mentor, even if he doesn't know it, as I've also said in previous principles.

By understanding the dynamics of money, which, depending on how you treat it, will either repay you or not, you will certainly change your life. That's why I highly recommend reading this book, as several times the author talks about this issue of double treatment, how each of his two fathers treated their own money. It's not for nothing that the name of the book is Rich Dad Poor Dad, because he considers two fathers, one rich and one poor, and in this way the author establishes this difference in business.

Moving on, it's important to remember the difference between saving and investing, because here in Brazil we talk a lot about saving, so much so that the best-known investment is savings. We worry a lot about saving, which is "putting money away". And where is this money going to stay? It's never made much difference, it's not a problem, the money can be in the drawer or even inside the mattress; there's even a classic soap opera, Amor com Amor Se Paga (1984), in which the character, Seu Nonô Correia, hid his money in a secret wall. I remember it perfectly because my mother used to call me Seu Nonô: the character in the 1980s soap opera was a tough guy who hid his money in a false wall. So we were brought up with this culture of saving, but there was little talk of investing, at most in land; everyone has an uncle who says "those who buy land don't make mistakes", at most that.

However, we need to turn that switch, from saving to investing. Of course, saving is much better than having debts, let me be clear here, at no point am I complaining if you are saving, I don't want you to pick up the book and think: "Charles criticized the act of saving, so I'm going to take and spend all the money in my drawer", because that's not what I'm talking about. What I'm saying is that, if we were to put it on a scale, the worst case scenario is debt, the good case scenario is saving and the best case scenario is investing.

You already have all the tools you need to learn how to invest, and when I say all the tools I only think of one: your brain. Do you have a brain, yes or no? If the answer is yes, you're ready to invest. What are you waiting for? Whether it's through this book, Rich Dad Poor Dad, other books, other courses... so, if money is your friend, run, embrace it and extract as much as you can.

Here's a very important point: once you've understood from what I've said that money is your friend, the best advice I can give you in this respect is: make money your childhood friend. What do I mean by that? The sooner you understand that money is your friend and change the way you deal with it, the better it will be for you. So let's take an example: imagine a young man in his twenties who gets out of debt, starts saving and then starts investing. And that's not all, because at the beginning of our lives we all - myself included - make mistakes when it comes to money, we treat this friend badly, when we don't treat it like an enemy, and what do I mean by treating it like an enemy? It's having card debts, a bad name... the sooner you sort this out and make money your childhood friend, the better.

There is a statistic in the world that more than 30% of lottery winners lose their money. Before you criticize them and laugh, I imagine that if I were standing next to you, you would say to me: "Well, Charles, they must be very stupid people, right?". But no, they're normal people like you and me, except that they've earned a lot of money and haven't learned to treat it as a friend.

I'll say it again: if you treat money as your childhood friend and learn to invest, you'll be prepared for any winnings, whether it's ten thousand, a hundred thousand, a million or ten million. The problem is with those who win a lottery jackpot, or sportspeople, for example, such as boxers or Brazilian soccer players, after all, why do these people lose so much money? Even reality show winners also lose a lot. This is because they don't know how to handle money, so it slips through their hands. Imagine a person who wins a million reais, as much as it seems like a lot of money, they buy a house for themselves, a house for their family, two cars and then lend the rest of the money to their friends, so they quickly look around and have no friends, no money and no family left. This is very common.

So what's the antidote? Learning to deal with money, treating it like your best friend, like a childhood friend, keeping it close to you. And then, once you've learned how to deal with R$5,000, you'll find it much easier to deal with R$50,000 or R$5 million. Around a third of lottery winners go bankrupt just a few years later, according to research carried out in the United States.

Once you've understood that money should be your friend, let's move on to the practical side. Anyone who follows my content on the internet through the videos, talks and lives I do knows that I insist that people start investing even with little money. When I say little, it's around R$20, R$40 or R$50. Now I'm going to tell you something in this book that I don't talk about much: why I do it this way. You already know that you have to start investing anyway, but deep down, it's precisely to remedy what I've been talking about in this chapter, which is that when I insist that you start investing with little money in any way, it's as if I'm at your side introducing you to money as a friend so that you can learn to deal with it as soon as possible.

If I could give you just one piece of advice on this principle, it would be: identify the stage you're at. Which of the three stages are you in? 1) Debt and financial problems? 2) Do you already save? 3) Do you already invest? Which of these stages are you in? It's important to identify your situation so that we can take the necessary steps if it's in your interest to change and improve your life.

If you have financial problems and debts, I suggest you pay everything off, don't think about anything else at this stage. Now is not the time to save and invest. I even think it's interesting that you start studying the subject, because sometimes R$20, R$30 won't make a difference, you can invest to get started, to feel good, as if you're taking a step forward, but it's important that you plug that drain. "But how?", you ask me, and I'll tell you that the way to do it will be to reduce expenses and renegotiate debts. It's very important that you stop, because I've never met anyone who has solved their financial problems by continuing without resolving past debts, because without doing so, you remain in debt, and you keep paying interest day after day.

So you're going to stop one day, sit down, organize, plan, renegotiate and then reset your life, start again. Everyone who just tries to solve their problems by staying in debt and letting the wheel spin won't get out of it, so much so that I know people who have had the same financial problems for twenty or thirty years and never find the time or conditions to stop and solve them. Curiously, these people never solve them, and why? It seems a bit obvious, but if you don't have the time or the conditions to stop and solve something, how can you solve it?

At this point, I'll say it again: if you can't live, save and invest with R$5,000, you won't be able to with R$5 million. If you don't understand this, you'll end up winning the Mega Sena or some reality TV show, or even becoming a famous sportsman, but you'll end up with no money at the end of your life. So, if you're having financial problems or are in debt, I advise you to finish the book, then stop in all areas of your life and make a new plan, after all, there's no shortage of online content for those who have this problem, right?

Now, there's a second point: if you're already in the savings phase, I have two things to say to you. Firstly, congratulations! You're already ahead of most Brazilians, maybe even the world's population. You're saving. So my first thing to say to you is congratulations; and the second, in reality, is a request, after all, why did you stop there? Why did you get to a stage that few people get to and not think about going further? Why do you have something in your hand that is so hard to come by, which is money, and do nothing to multiply it? Money sitting idle also causes mold.

So I suggest you learn to invest immediately, because the main input for your financial success is money, and you already have it. Why aren't you improving your life? Why aren't you putting your money to work for you? What's the point? Have you ever stopped to think that the money you have sitting idle, if well invested in the short, medium and long term, could bring you, for example, a monthly minimum wage and income? And that a minimum wage, for many people, means waking up at six o'clock in the morning, taking a bus for two hours, going to work, not eating properly, putting up with a boss that nobody likes, taking another bus back from work for two hours, getting home and doing all the household chores and only having time to sleep until this cycle starts again? Many people end their lives to earn a minimum wage and it's so possible to do this with money working for you, it's hard to understand why nobody stops and learns.

But I'll say it again, the hardest thing of all is that you already have the money and, in principle, it seems to me that you also have a brain. So you can already learn to invest. What's missing? Just one thing in the equation: will.

The third and final stage, which is also the best, is the stage in which you no longer have debts and financial problems, have managed to save and have learned how to invest, regardless of whether you are a beginner, intermediate or advanced investor. You might be thinking: "Well, Charlão's going to congratulate me now!". Well, I could congratulate you, but that would only massage your ego, and I'm not here to soften anyone up. I'm here to take you beyond where you would have gone on your own, just as they did with me during this process. So I have some advice for you if you're already invested.

First, beware of overconfidence. Respect your time, i.e. if you are an investor who has been in the market for two years, is making a lot of money and thinks that your financial life will be like this, without knowing your case I can already tell you that you have probably simply caught a high tide, a market that is rising strongly. It's very common to start losing money, so do you know how long your journey as an investor will take? A lifetime, because it's constant learning. You've already done the hardest part, and I might even rethink congratulating you on what I didn't do, so I'll do it now, but I'm going to say it quietly, because I don't want it to go to your head and for you to lose your money on scams, on investments that clearly weren't interesting, but seemed very good. So, start investing, increase your knowledge, understand that this is for life, focus your investment on assets that generate an income, as you can see and learn from the book Rich Dad Poor Dad.

Now, never let your guard down. Investing is also about being alert, because making money is difficult, but losing money on investments is very easy, in a matter of minutes you can lose a lifetime of sacrifices. So my congratulations are very measured.

Principle

Always use time to your advantage

With all of life's injustices, you've become an adult and you should have gotten used to the fact that life really isn't fair, but if there's one thing that practically everyone gets in equal measure and which, curiously, is the most important part of everything, it's time.

We could spend the whole book discussing the issue of time, after all, what is more important, if time is money, time is knowledge, time is health? It would be a pleasure to sit here and discuss it with you, but my conclusion, and that of most people, is that time is the most valuable thing we have, and why? Because it's finite. So practically everyone comes to Earth with an hourglass that's dripping sand counting down ⍰⍰.⍰⍰⍰ days.

What would those 36,500 days be? A year has 365 days, you're probably going to live a hundred years, so when the doctor slapped you on the ass and you started crying, in the first minute of life you started complaining, your stopwatch also started spinning: 36,500, 36,499, 36,498, 36,497... and so on.

So every day, no matter what you do, you lose a day. That's not going to change, it works like that for me, for you, for Bill Gates, for the guy in prison... for everyone it's going to be exactly the same. "Gee, Charles, but I know someone who has a disease and lives less", fine, you're taking an exception, but I'm saying that, in general, we have these 36,500 days.

Every day that we don't use to our advantage is something that we're wasting and that won't come back. How many times in the same lifetime does a person gain and lose money, gain and lose something else, lose weight and put on weight? They can change many things, but the only thing that doesn't change is that every day you have one less day. So, if you don't use that day to your advantage, you'll damage the rest of your life and just by wasting your days you'll have wasted valuable time for nothing. How many people spend five, ten, fifteen, twenty years living a mediocre life, wasting time that won't come back and knowing that, often, from the middle of life onwards, some of our capacities diminish for reasons of health, speed, cognitive ability?

So the first point you have to understand in this principle is that you should use the time you've been given as well as possible and as soon as possible, because while you're reading this book, you've also put in a few hours, but at least I hope they've been productive. This is the first point of the 36,500 days. It's like a stopwatch that's running, whether you like it or not.

If you're over thirty, you might be thinking at this point: "Well, Charles, but I've used up a lot of that 36,500-day reservoir in a non-productive way and now I'm at a disadvantage compared to someone who still has a lot of time and more knowledge than me"; this is partly true, and I'm not going to pull your leg. If you've spent your time in your thirties, forties, fifties or even sixties, you really can't go back in time, but we can deal with that later. However, some people have already proved that by understanding that you've done little so far, you may have learned that from now on you'll have to speed up more than others.

There are countless success stories, and I myself have come across people in their fifties, sixties and seventies who were successful and started "late". One example is Henri Nestlé himself, who invented dairy flour at the age of 52, creating a successful company that I'm sure you're familiar with. Another well-known case is that of the inventor of Coca-Cola, a pharmacist, who discovered the product originally as a medicine for stomach pains at the age of 55. There's also the creator of the KFC fast-food chain, who only achieved success with his chain of restaurants at the age of 65, i.e. 25 years after opening the first KFC. The owner of this famous fast-food chain, Colonel Sanders, didn't sell his first franchise until he was 62. To finish off this list, another super-famous case is that of Ray Kroc, who is well chronicled in the movie Hunger for Power. He started the fast-food chain model at the age of 52.

So if you're over thirty, forty or fifty, don't expect me to be sensitive to any concerns you might have about your age. What matters is what you do from now on, not what you did in the past, because, as I said at the beginning of this principle, everything can be resolved, except the time that has passed, because that won't come back. So if you don't change your attitude, tomorrow is just another day you've lost.

In the 1960s, psychologist Walter Mischel decided to develop a test to assess children's level of self-control. This test became known as the "marshmallow test", although the researcher also used other sweets. He let the participants choose the sweet they liked best, which could be chocolate, ice cream, candy, cookies... Then the child was taken to a room, seated in a chair in front of a table. The child's favorite candy was placed on the table, then he told the child that he would leave the room and leave him alone with the candy; if he didn't eat the candy, he would get another one when the psychologist returned. If she wanted to, she could eat the candy, but then she wouldn't get any more.

So the researcher left the room, but can you imagine how the child felt in front of a delicious sweet? This experiment has been repeated by other researchers in more recent times and some of them are available in videos on the internet. The recent videos of the experiment demonstrate exactly the pattern of behavior seen by Mischel back in the 1960s. Some participants started eating the candy before the researcher even left the room, others managed to control themselves, sometimes with great effort. Some children even used the strategy of sniffing the candy or taking small pieces at a time in an attempt to resist. For children, this sacrifice is great because of their level of cognitive maturity, and a few minutes of being deprived of pleasure can seem like an eternity.

When the researcher returned to the room, he gave the second candy to those who hadn't eaten the first, in other words, a reward for those who managed to act with self-control. The main issue surrounding the experiment is self-control and the benefits; the children knew that they could enjoy the benefit of double the candy if they controlled themselves.

The difficulty is that the momentary pleasure ends up taking away from the person the later benefit. However, the most important thing is that this experiment shows, through these children, that people often forget the issue of time. They prefer a momentary pleasure to a lasting benefit down the line. So, what for children is a marshmallow, a sweet, a candy, a double Coca-Cola, for most people doesn't enter into the rat race story I talked about when quoting the book Rich Dad Poor Dad? I mean, if you earn five thousand, would you rather spend it all, buy everything you can, instead of investing it and enjoying it in three or four years?

So when I tell you to use time to your advantage, it's also to understand that you have these 36,500 days, but be careful, because if you don't prepare yourself halfway through, you won't have any resources or good living conditions. So it's very important that you learn, seek knowledge, prepare yourself, but that you also think about what your life will be like from now on, if you're not anticipating your dreams and killing your future. Isn't your present costing you your future?

Knowledge is priceless, so if you say to me: "Well, Charles, but I've been spending a lot. I've been eating my marshmallow, but my marshmallow has been knowledge", then I'm willing to argue with you. Not anything else, because it's this knowledge that has the power to multiply your earning potential. But what's wrong with the whole knowledge thing? I know several people who take various courses throughout the year, always looking for knowledge, but never apply any of it. In fact, they don't even need knowledge anymore. So be careful, because sometimes it's the fear of things working out that gets in the way; you just study and don't put anything into practice.

Of course, there are debatable cases, so if someone says to you: "Oh, I earn five thousand, but I'm spending 2.5 thousand on a fucking MBA that's very expensive...", that's fine, then we can discuss it, because you're not buying a car, but investing in something that might double your salary.

There's also the question of "I deserve it", but this is very problematic. I'm a great believer in our prosperity, and I myself say that you have to give yourself things, have small goals and everything, but there are a lot of disloyal people using what I say and inverting or distorting these ideas. I'll give you an example here, let's say you started your own business, in which you had a goal of making R$100,000 a month, and then you made R$150,000. And imagine that, in this scenario, you want to go out with two friends and pay for a great steakhouse for them, totally within reason. After all, you're working.

Or, for example, some influencer who sold a million on the course and is looking to buy a twenty-thousand-dollar watch. That's not what I'm talking about, I'm referring to people who have the following thought: "Oh... I've had a super stressful day, I hate my boss", they haven't had a raise or anything, but they think: "I hate my boss. I'm going to call all my friends for lunch and that's it, I deserve it". Yes, you deserve it. You deserve the condition you're in and can't get out of.

You've already understood that time is finite, that it's against you, and that you must seek knowledge, but you can't anticipate your dreams, your pleasures, like children anticipate marshmallows. There's also a very important point: when, at the beginning of this principle, I talked about people wasting five or fifteen years, I've wasted a lot of time too, not with deep depression, but sometimes we enter a time limbo in which one, two, five, ten years go by and we don't evolve, we get stuck in certain feelings, things don't happen... whether in relationships, work or finances. When we look back, years have passed and we don't know where that time has gone, it's like money disappearing. Time also disappears in our hands and that's why we need to talk about two important things: anxiety and depression.

I'm not going to go too deeply into these topics at the moment, but we can link the issue of sadness and depression to the past, to things that have happened that you haven't forgiven yourself for or that you haven't forgiven the other person for. But if you don't seek help to heal this sadness and depression that are related to your past, it will consume the days of your future, and then the account won't close. If I've told you that you have 36,500 days, you know that your hourglass has a hole in it, it's leaking sand, more than it should, so you need to plug that hole. "Well, Charlão, I've been depressed for years, I can't solve it". If you can't manage on your own, you'll have to take other measures, in other words, you'll have to seek help, whether it's professional or even through meditation, but you need to plug this hole, because your timer is spinning faster this way.

So, if you have depression or deep sadness linked to things that have happened in your life, you'll have to stop and sort it out, because otherwise your time will count faster than everyone else's.

Your past will consume the days of your future.

Most people don't know where they are. What have you done in the last five years that is significant in your life? "I've done nothing", why haven't you done anything? "Oh, man, let me tell you the truth? I used to work for a company like this, this and this, nobody valued me, I got fired and now I don't do anything anymore". Ah, so because they treated you like shit, you turned into shit? You were a good person, a good worker, they didn't value you, they fired you and, instead of you revolutionizing your life by proving that you weren't that, you became exactly that?

"Oh, I don't stay after hours anymore," but why don't you stay after hours anymore? "I already stayed one day and they didn't appreciate me," you mean you were a good professional and then they treated you like a bad professional and you became a bad professional? It doesn't make any sense. So congratulations to those who fired you, they only anticipated who you would become, you could have become that within the guys' own company, they had the vision, they looked at you and thought: "This guy isn't a good professional, he's a bad professional playing the role of a good professional, but in a little while he'll become a bad professional", and that's what you became.

Although focusing our attention on past events is important, this is not a book that deals only with the past and, as I've said on several occasions, what matters is your life from now on. When we talk about the future, there is an evil that plagues everyone, including me, and that is anxiety. So sadness and depression are very much linked to the past, while anxiety is linked to the future.

We live in constant worry about tomorrow, after all, what will happen tomorrow? What will happen next year? What will happen in ten years' time? Society also makes us worry about goals. I myself, in this book, have asked you several times to make your goals, and this generates anxiety. But is that bad? So worrying about the future has been necessary since the time of the caves, we had to worry about what we were going to eat the next day, where we were going to be, whether we were going to be able to reproduce...

In this way, worrying is an important part of what you have to do. However, if you worry too much, are too anxious and it makes it impossible for you to take action, your future won't exist.

So these feelings need to be on your radar, because throughout your life, at various times, you will have these sensations that you need to protect yourself from, but how? By shedding light, by being aware. By being aware of "I'm sad", "I'm depressed", "I'm anxious", you've already gone halfway, because you've identified the problem, and can therefore solve it. That's it. What are you anxious about? Are you short of money? Are you not progressing in your job?

And now that we've discussed the issue of time, you're going to live - and I hope you'll live past that - 36,500 days. But to wrap up this principle, I'd like to point out one last thing: if your time is already estimated, every day that passes is one less day in your life. So how about making better use of that time over the next few days?

To do this, I have a few suggestions; you don't have to follow them, but if you want to, you can start doing them. I'll give you an example: you can spend an hour of your time at the gym, an hour of your time listening to a podcast, and another hour of your time monitoring your health so that you drink two liters of water, but do you want to know what's most interesting? You can do all three things at the same time. So why not do an hour of exercise every day, listen to a podcast or something useful and still drink something healthy? Do you agree with me that you're optimizing your time with something that will probably bring you more results and perhaps even more time, if all goes well?

For a few years, I didn't make the best use of my time, but today I do. So, when I'm doing the dishes, training at the gym, taking a shower, when I'm doing any of these tasks, I have my cell phone next to a podcast or a video that will help me get where I want to go.

"Gee, Charles, but I feel good doing the treadmill while listening to a song", that's fine, I feel fine too, I often listen to a song, but is just listening to a song going to get you where you want to go? Don't just do what you like, do what you need to do.

I'm not saying that every time you go to the gym, wash dishes, go for a walk with your dog... that time needs to be 100% productive, but stop and think with me here, if you start to make a habit of, in some moments you do some activity that allows you to add something constructive like studying and learning something new, it's already much better than doing nothing. I also like to listen to music or watch a joke video, but I try to make my time as productive as possible.

I'd also like to say that it's all about balance. Because, for example, even when you do mental hygiene by distracting yourself, reducing your stress levels, you're also optimizing your time. When I start a workout in the morning, louder music usually helps energize me. Then I start to reason, think, come up with various ideas, even develop some content, and you know why? My brain is exploding, so it's precisely the moment I take advantage of to absorb information from different sources, because I already have my knowledge, but it's finite. When we have our knowledge, plus a positive emotional charge and the knowledge of others, we form a melting pot of ideas.

Now that we've talked about how finite and special your time is, let's make the best use of it. And as I proposed in other principles, let's try an improvement exercise here? Let's imagine that in the last few days you've done nothing, in other words, in the last few months you haven't listened to a podcast related to your area of work or the area you want to learn, you haven't watched any educational videos on YouTube, you haven't read a book. So how about setting yourself the challenge of trying to combine the two into one this week? In other words, when you walk your dog, you'll listen to a podcast. When you wash the dishes, you'll watch a YouTube video with some new learning or knowledge. Try to improve on at least one point this week.

I don't like mentors, gurus, teachers who try to take you from zero to a hundred in two seconds, and you know why? Because it will only last two seconds. Here we're working on continuous improvement, where the impact of what we're sharing in this book will last every day of your life. So don't worry about going from zero to a hundred in two seconds, worry about going a hundred kilometers an hour in a while so that you never stop. That makes a lot more sense, right?

I'm not worried about that "how many books have you read in the last five years?" thing. You haven't read any? Then I want you to read at least one this year. "Oh, you have to read ten", no fucking way! Man, it's habit, it's constancy and consistency.

If I don't read part of a book in a week I go crazy, because it's become a habit for me..

15

Principle

Use the orbit effect
and change levels

What is the concept of "Use the orbit effect and change levels"? So far in this book, we've talked about many points that can help a person evolve, be it in reading, in friendships, in the family or with a spouse, in various areas of life. But there's a small problem: nobody wants to evolve so that in forty years' time they'll be fine; they want to evolve soon, you and I want to evolve soon, everyone wants to evolve soon. Mainly because we want to make up for lost time, so if you haven't read any books in the last thirty years, now you think you're going to read all the books in the next twelve months, but life unfortunately doesn't work like that.

What conclusion can we draw? The conclusion is that it is possible to evolve, but there's another important point: how fast? In this principle, we're going to address the question of how fast you want to evolve, to get where you want to go, but above all, how long you want to stay there. There are those clichés that say it's easy to get to the top of a mountain, but difficult to stay there.

Let's imagine that you've already made the decision and, if you've got as far as this beginning of the book, it's possible that you'll continue, because by now you've made the decision to change your life, to evolve, to improve a little bit every day, but you've also decided to speed up this process, which is great, especially if you've lost some time. I like to compare life to an airplane flight and, if you've ever taken a flight, you know or should know that airplanes consume a lot of fuel and need a lot of power to keep flying, especially those with two, three or four turbines. It's consuming a lot of fuel and, if the engines stop, it will probably crash, at most it will glide a little and then crash. So what conclusion can we draw? Either the plane burns a lot of fuel and flies, or it stops burning fuel and immediately starts to descend; that's an airplane.

Life can be compared to an airplane, because we wake up, go to the gym, have to work, study, solve problems at home, and in all this we burn a lot of fuel. Well, what if I decided to stop burning fuel and do nothing else?

Just like an airplane, you're going to crash. If you woke up and decided to tell your boss to fuck off, you'd probably have to find another job in the next few weeks or months, just as if you threw an apple at your professor at university, you'd be expelled, you'd have to make up for it. What I'm trying to say here in detail is exactly that, your life is nothing more than an airplane burning an enormous amount of energy every day and you can't stop. The worst thing is that society makes us into mediocre people. Mediocre, here, is used to refer to people who are average, it's not a slur - although I think "average" is a slur, and I wouldn't want anyone to say I'm average. The longer we live life in a mediocre way, the more fuel we burn and we can't stop.

One proof of this is that many of us despair when we're sick and can't work, for fear that someone will replace us, send us away, and it even becomes a common habit for people not to take vacations for fear that someone else might take their place, but why is that? Because you have this notion, consciously or unconsciously, that you're an airplane burning energy all the time.

"Well, Charlão, I understand and agree with that, but is it possible to be different?" That's the point, it is possible to be different. By studying the lives of multimillionaires, billionaires, and my own life experiences and personal experiences, I was able to identify a format, a series of attitudes that can make you lead a different life. Society says that you have to burn energy all the time or you'll fall down, and now I'm telling you this: you can be different from that. However, there is a small problem, which is that at first it will get much worse before it gets better. Do you agree? That's the big question.

Now, what's the other proposal? What I've identified and seen with billionaires, reading, experiencing, seeing my successful bosses, my unsuccessful bosses, friends, family and all that, is that there is another format which, if we compare it to the story of the airplane, would be that of a rocket. Unlike the airplane, the rocket burns a lot of energy, much more, for a short time, but what does it do? It puts a satellite into orbit around the Earth. It burns more energy and the risks are greater, of an explosion, of it not working, in other words, there are a lot of problems and you burn a lot more energy, but when a satellite is put into orbit, when something leaves the Earth, you no longer need to burn energy.

What I'm saying here is that you can lead a mediocre life for ten, fifteen, twenty, thirty years and keep burning energy like an airplane, but I have a different proposal: for the next five years, you'll burn much more energy than anyone else, but you'll reach orbit and that orbit will allow you to stop, and get your time back.

For example, if I wanted to stop working for a year, I could, why? Because I'm in orbit, I'm no longer in an airplane burning energy. Now, here are a lot of people my age, 46, who don't have any money, probably because from their twenties to their thirties they didn't work for a living, didn't want to do an MBA, didn't want to teach in college, didn't want to have extra income, didn't want to travel for work... and so on.

I've had friends turn to me, back when I used to travel and sleep anywhere, and say: "If I have to travel for work, the company has to pay for a better hotel than my house, because I'm not going to work and sleep in a place that's worse than my house". What's that, big guy? It's okay, if you think it has to be that way, fine. I've slept in a car, but what you want is up to you.

This orbit effect gives you a chance to take responsibility, to speed up a little now so that you can get your time back. What does it take? A greater energy burn. You're going to push yourself, instead of working X amount of time in fifteen, twenty years, you're going to do it in five, and you're going to burst, you might even explode. That's why we need to have some controls, your instruments. You can't help but look after your health, as well as taking care of burnout. The better your diet, the better you look after your body, the less chance there is of your rocket exploding. So what do you have to do now? Synchronize the two, because yes, it is possible to accelerate, as long as you prepare your structure, your rocket version.

It's important to point out that at some point during your life you're going to have a controlled imbalance. I'd like to say that I'm not encouraging anyone to have a burnout, although if you have the opportunity to talk to successful people, there's probably practically zero chance that they haven't worked hard over a period of time. So beware of false gurus who preach balance when, in fact, their lives are unbalanced.

There are some very dangerous gurus, I'd go so far as to say it's criminal what they do when they say: "Oh, you have to balance everything in life", and you notice in their lives something super unbalanced, travel, work, etc.

While I'm saying "you have to work harder and dedicate yourself", a "false guru" appears, or someone else who says: "I'll sell you my course for

R$1,997.00 so that you can learn to balance your life", but there's no such thing. Life has no shortcuts.

This is because they say what people want to hear. Popping the pill is something that brings comfort to our brains, which like to be fooled. An example of this is the person who is very overweight and who, instead of listening to me, opens the channel to a sedentary person who will say: "You have to feel good about who you are and the way you are". I'm not saying that we don't have to feel good about ourselves, but that this person has to take care of themselves and improve, while the other guy is just saying: "Be sedentary and happy".

I want to make it clear that I don't want to encourage burnout, on the contrary; I've been through it a few times, but I really don't see a simplified, pretty way for you to grow both in a company and in your business, leaving everything "balanced". If you decide to balance the plates, I'm sorry to tell you, but you'll only be able to do it with very few plates. There's no miracle.

So what can you do to make sure things don't get out of hand? Take care of yourself, sleep well, take care of your diet, have regular check-ups, seek help... many successful people also end up being successful in a sport, because doing some physical activity in parallel will help you a lot to get through this phase.

Eight recommendations for achieving the Orbit Effect

With all this in mind, I'm going to give you eight recommendations to help you achieve the orbit effect in the best possible way.

Recommendation n°. 1: Stop wasting time watching nothing. Watching a lot of TV, in other words, waking up and turning it on, hunting for something to watch at weekends, zapping the channels at night before going to sleep is an old habit of older people, from my age upwards... It is essential that people change this habit for something that is a little more in line with what they want, with their goals. I don't know what your goal is, but I can assure you that if you have this habit, which I once had, you need to sort it out. Don't waste any more time watching TV. "Well, Charles, but I use that TV time to watch Telecurso 2000 and learn a new profession". So ok, use the TV, and you can even double the time, otherwise, stop procrastinating.

Recommendation n°. 2: Use your time usefully. If you're from the new generation that enjoys streaming and also this new world of podcasts, as I've said before, I need you to make the most of your time, so make the most of your weekends and your day-to-day so that you can see things that will make a difference to your life. Whatever your job, the amount of material you have today is enormous on these platforms, on YouTube itself, for example. You need to immediately make notes, search for this material, organize a way to see all the useful content you can in the coming months. From paid content on Netflix to free content on YouTube, knowledge is available like never before.

Remember how I talked about the issue of mediocrity? By doing this, you're already positioning yourself differently from most people, so I'm trying to get you out of the mediocrity line.

Recommendation n°. 3: Use social media wisely. Social media. I'm suspicious because I'm a social media enthusiast, so I would never use this book to speak ill of it. Unlike many people, I don't think that social media is destroying humanity, damaging everything; of course the algorithms have ended up creating bubbles, and these bubbles often lead to extremism, but there is also the positive side of social media. If you've already defined your plan, you know your purpose, you know where you want to go, let's harness the power of social media for that. So, are you using social media in the right way or do you pick up your cell phone every ten minutes to enjoy a picture of your ass?

But how can we use social media in the right way? According to our goals, just as I just talked to you about Netflix. I'm not asking you to become an alien and no longer have the habits that everyone else has; I'm just asking you to align those habits with your goals. Or do you think it won't make any difference for you to consume all the possible materials on the subject you want to evolve? I don't see anything harmful in you being the most knowledgeable in your field, whether you're a CLT or an entrepreneur.

It's very bizarre to imagine that there are people who want to evolve in a certain segment and don't consume content about it, or do you think you're going to evolve from the inside out? Without consuming content? That's idiotic. I believe you can evolve on your own, but what a stupid thing to do: you want to develop your own theories when, many times, they've already been developed. So, by ignoring the knowledge that's available in the world, you're wasting a huge amount of time.

Recommendation n°. 4: Exercise. I'm tackling a very delicate subject here, which I'm sure will or could lead many people to burnout, but there's no way I want that to happen. So try, just do it and give it your best shot, try as much as possible to include exercise in your routine, at least three times a week. "Well, Charles, I can't include exercise three times a week", then change your routine or it will go wrong. I don't know your life, I'm not a prophet, but I guarantee that what you're doing will go wrong. If they can't fit anything in, they can take a step back and redo their routine. What makes someone think they can't devote thirty minutes to a workout, some physical activity, some sport?

What I can suggest for you is to think about some physical exercise that you can do close to home, close to work or close to your school or college. If you wait until you get home from work to change your clothes, sort something out and go out, it's not going to work, especially if you have to take the bus, get in the car...

Getting into the habit of waking up early can also help make it work. Let's think about it: nobody usually starts work or school at six in the morning, but the gym is already open at that time. Or just think about walking down the street... anything. So give preference to exercising early in the morning, for me it makes a lot of difference. I also prefer it at the start of the day, I feel good at the start of the day, and science has proven that.

Stop wasting time thinking about problems that have already been solved.

Recommendation n°. 5: Take care of your diet. We don't want your rocket to stop halfway because the fuel is adulterated, which, by the way, leads me to think about how I myself, for a long time, made mistakes that are inexplicable. If we knew of a gas station that used adulterated fuel, we would never stop to fill up at it. In other words, we don't want to ruin our car, but we ruin our body every day by eating badly. I'm not going to set myself up as "Lord Food" or the guy who has the most perfect diet in the world, but over the last few years I've learned to respect my body and so I avoid ultra-processed foods, eat salad every day and drink at least two liters of water a day. These are small habits that guarantee a healthy diet.

There are many people who find excuses for everything, from "I don't like it" to "Oh, but I don't have time to eat well, to cook...". There are thousands of people who don't even eat fruit, but in Brazil they don't have this excuse. If we lived like this in the USA, where hamburgers are US$1 and there's more scarcity of this type of food, ok, but in Brazil? Are you crazy? In any sacolão you'll find a huge variety of fruit, a well-made PF or a restaurant per kilo where you can choose what you want.

Recommendation n°. 6: Kill the difficult tasks. It's very important that you don't put off the most difficult tasks of everyday life, because this kills your productivity. And why does it kill your productivity? Because it's something that stays in your head, takes up time, generates negative emotions and gives you the idea of being overloaded. Having too many tasks pending, especially difficult ones that you don't like doing, only makes you procrastinate a lot and this completely disrupts your day. Trust me, I say this because it's happened to me.

And what's the solution? Simple, a pad of paper and a pen, if possible get them both now. Funnily enough, I don't know if you've seen any of my videos on YouTube, but I have a raffle where the prize is a book and a notepad; now, have you ever wondered why the notepad goes with it? The pad goes along so that people can organize their lives in the same way I organize mine. It's so simple that even a huge procrastinator won't be able to give me an excuse, or can't you have a pad and pen?

I assume I'm "Mr. Pen and Paper", so how do I start my day? I always write down what I have to do that day, and then I cross off the tasks as I complete them. This ritual begins as soon as I get up, because I'm already thinking about how my day will go, analyzing the tasks I'll have throughout the day, as well as any unfinished business from the day before. I also always start the day with a blank page, unless I have previously scheduled appointments.

Write this suggestion down on your list, and you can choose any way you like to organize it. However, one of the best known is the Eisenhower matrix. This is a good strategy so that you don't get the feeling that you have a whole elephant in front of you, and then you think: "Damn, I'm not going to be able to swallow it all in one go".

Eisenhower matrix

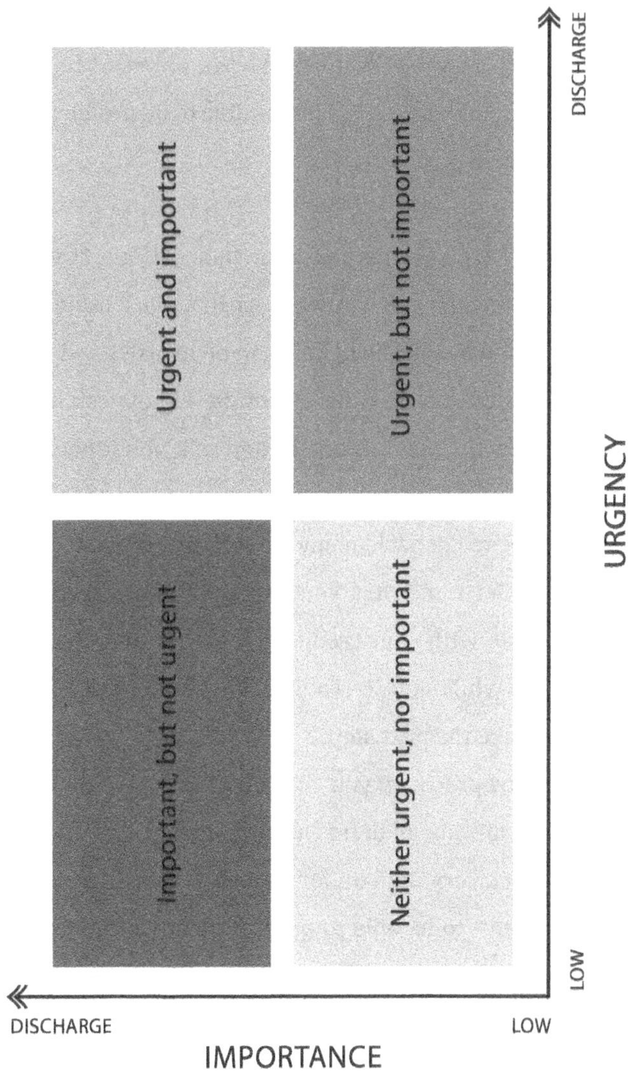

As you can see, you can separate: what is important but not urgent; what is urgent and important; what is neither urgent nor important; and what is urgent but not important.

Just one last point, I like to use a pen and pad, but if a post it note is better for you, or if you use an online planner like Notion, that's fine, what you can't do is get lost without planning, it's impossible to be productive without a minimum organizational structure.

Recommendation n°. 7: Reorganize your financial life. If you want to make a much bigger leap than average, work harder, reach orbit and be able to stop, have a different life, your head needs to be in order and nobody can perform very well when their life is disorganized. I know you'll remember a lot of entrepreneurs who give interviews and talk about how they went broke but then got back on their feet, and you might even be thinking: "I'm broke too and I'm going to get back on my feet", that's fine, you can get back on your feet, but in order to do that, you first have to organize yourself. If you're having a problem with your credit card, if your account is a bit of a mess, stop, right now, while you're reading this book, reorganize your finances, then you can take the next step.

Those broken entrepreneurs you find out there, yes, they've broken down, I've even talked to some of them, but they've reorganized themselves so that life can go on. It's very difficult for a person with a disorganized life, full of financial problems, to be able to prosper, because even if it's sunny, you always have a cloud over your head when you have financial problems. Often you'll be with your family, everyone in a good moment, in a moment of happiness, but you won't be completely happy, or even present, because you're having that financial problem.

I'm not asking you to solve the problem overnight, because these problems often take time. I'm just asking you to organize ways of solving the problem, and then you can speed things up.

Recommendation n°. 8: Don't be motivated, be disciplined. You're probably thinking that this was written wrong in the book, because it should read "be motivated", but no. I'm asking you not to be motivated. I'm asking you not to be motivated at all. That's because, if you want to get into orbit, get out of this fuel-burning life and have a better life more quickly, motivation can help you at first, but the word for it isn't motivation, it's discipline.

So I don't give a damn how motivated you are to make your life work; right now, I need you to be committed, to have discipline, because if you're motivated to change and a difficulty arises tomorrow, you'll stop being motivated. Now, if you're committed and disciplined, when the first difficulty arises, you'll understand that it's a passing difficulty, and that you still have to keep going.

It's very important that you understand the difference between motivation, discipline and commitment. To get further, you don't need motivation ALONE; motivation is very nice, it's beautiful. If you want to shout "I'm a fucker" every morning, I'm not against it, but for the place you want to get to, there's no one who got there without discipline. I know millionaires who have often been discouraged for various reasons, but I don't know any millionaires without discipline and commitment.

Motivation is that thing, isn't it? The coach says: "Come on, everyone, 'I'm a fucker!'", then the person shivers and shouts: "I'm a fucker!". Then Monday comes, "the egg's gone, José, you have to buy the egg", "have you walked the dog yet?", "I haven't, what the fuck!". In two days you're no longer a fuck-up. It's over. That's why people go to these coaching events and their lives don't change at all.

Now, if you draw up a plan: "I'm going to do this, that, go to college, start working, make an extra income, buy some products and sell them on the free market...". If the guy creates a plan, follows something nice, is committed and disciplined, it doesn't matter.

Is motivation cool? It's cool and I'm not against motivation, I think it's important to be motivated. I'm not against motivation, but do you know what motivation will do in this orbit thing? At most, it will make your rocket start on fire. But what will put you into orbit is discipline and commitment. Commitment to yourself, which means that even if something goes wrong, you'll keep going.

This difference between commitment, discipline and motivation is super important, because this excitement doesn't last forever. You can see how many people are excited at first, but then what? I'll give you a concrete example: many people ask me for advice on starting a YouTube channel, and since my channel is successful they ask me: "Hey, Charlão, how do you start a YouTube channel?", and as always, I answer the same things. I stop for a while, sit down and explain how it works: just as important as quality is consistency on the platform, which is why you need two to three videos a week on the same day, at the same time. The problem is that the very "excited" and very motivated person thanks me, but then goes on with their life.

I like to follow these developments, and what usually happens? The person starts a channel and a few months later the channel is abandoned, but why? Because at the beginning of YouTube it's very difficult for your channel to do well, you spend all your energy on that initial motivation, but you forget the main piece of advice I gave you, which wasn't about how to get started, but about being consistent and disciplined. However, the person has no consistency, and why? Because their motivation is gone, so they're no longer excited about their channel. So if you don't know the difference between motivation, discipline and commitment, you won't be able to evolve.

16

Principle

Be curious and understand the world

If you've made it this far, you'll have noticed that I value documentaries and knowledge in general. And if you follow me, you'll know that I'm very fond of wine, cigars, culture in general, travel... And speaking of travel, have you ever wondered why every millionaire travels all the time? Is it just to post pictures on Instagram? Or is there something behind it? I can answer that for you, as life has allowed me to meet these millionaires in person.

And if you're wondering, at the beginning of my professional life, I had a few bosses who ended up being mentors and career gurus; I also found it very strange that they wanted to travel all the time. Today, being on the other side of the coin, that is, on the side of the millionaires, I can say that it's not just a question of luxury, pleasure, cuisine... it may be, in part, but the reality is that money can give you something unique: access to different cultures. KNOWLEDGE DOESN'T TAKE UP SPACE.

As I said before, until the early 2000s, access to information depended a lot on geography, because there was a geographical barrier. So, if I wanted to learn about Japanese or Chinese culture, or the way Americans eat, I had to go there. Nowadays, you know that the internet gives us a wealth of information.

Where do you want to go? Is it possible, from your home, to have access to the same information as millionaires, have you ever stopped to think about that? That the information that is available to Bill Gates, to Warren Buffett, is also available to you? And then I ask you, what are you doing with this information? Or did you not even realize it?

A brain that expands never returns to its original state.

That said, the idea of this principle, that you should be curious and understand the world, is that you should open up your horizons. Around 99% of the information you need is free, because it's already available on the internet. So you don't have a single reason not to succeed, because it's exactly when you look at this information that you run the risk of succeeding.

Now come on, telling yourself that millionaires travel, enjoy and seek out new cultures won't help you at first. That's why I'm going to share some advice that I've used in the past and that can help you evolve.

First of all: study as many topics as possible linked to the content you want to succeed in. I've already talked to you a bit about this, but I suggest that you take a piece of paper and a pen - it could be the same pad you use for your assignments - and write it down. Not on the computer, with pen and paper, because that makes a lot of difference. Write down everything you can get your hands on in terms of free information related to the area you want to develop. For example, if you're in the food industry, what documentaries are there? What programs? What movies? What can take you further, what is part of your segment, that you haven't seen yet?

For example, if you're in sales, there's a wealth of documentary material, films, biographies of great salespeople, sales lessons - have you seen them all? If you haven't, what are you waiting for? Because we have another problem, remember when I said that today the geographical barrier has fallen? That's very nice, but it also causes a problem for you, and you know what it is? A problem that has arisen for everyone, not just you. The point is that if you want to thrive in a segment, your competitors may be looking at the part of your segment that you're not looking at and studying.

The positive side is that you can improve a lot; however, the negative side is that your competitors can also improve and, in this race, those who are the most prepared and disciplined will get further. So study - write down and study - as many subjects as you can.

Second part of the same concept: look for subjects you like. This is important, so look for subjects that you like, write down a maximum of three and study them over the next few years. I'll give you my example: I've loved history, wine and cigars for years, and anyone who follows me on social media knows that I've delved into these subjects, mostly for free; but since I already have a background, in the case of wine, for example, I trained as a sommelier and obtained international certifications during my quest for knowledge. "Well, Charles, but how can studying these subjects without any connection to your main purpose help?" Everything! When I started studying more about history, wine and cigars, I expanded my horizons. I'm telling you all the time that knowledge doesn't take up space, and that knowledge will help you go further.

Now, when we manage to combine knowledge with something we like, it's much easier to evolve. When I find myself studying wine, I end up studying history, entrepreneurship, wars, culture, within a theme that I like. Therefore, separating everything you can from a subject you want to work on, evolving, and looking for three subjects that have to do with something you like, will certainly take you further.

I'll help you, do you like soccer? Who has won all the World Cups? Which countries? What are the stories behind these countries? Who were the great players? Which wars took place during the major World Cups? Which countries couldn't participate in World Cups because there were wars? Do you know about them?

"Well, Charles, I don't like soccer, but I like other sports"; in that case, have you looked into the Olympics? Do you know what happened at the Munich Olympics, about the attacks? Did they happen or not - did we or did we not have Olympics during the world's great wars? Have you looked into this?

It's not just about world knowledge, it's also about how you make yourself more interesting, even so that you can achieve other things. They become interesting for a new job, a circle of friends, a relationship. That's because when a person is drained of content, they become very uninteresting.

That said, take notes on three topics that are not related to your work, so you already have four topics. You don't have to study all three, my intention is that you don't even study all three at once, select one and study it, two, three and study it, but don't go beyond three, otherwise you'll continue to know nothing about any topic. Try to start with what you like best, whether it's soccer, wine, whisky or beer, then you can even add how much interesting information we have about beer, the main producers, what is used, the stories, the monks who started it all...

A very interesting point is that by studying all of this, topics linked to what you want and what you like, have you ever stopped to think that you will become a more complete and more interesting person, both professionally and personally? And don't you think that being a better person will help you go further? This is very important, because I realize that people often live in a state of scarcity because they leave their mental field too empty, without taking care of themselves and without coming up with interesting ideas. Have you ever heard that? "Oh, I can't think of anything". But the problem was still what I was talking about in past theories. People believe that they're going to evolve on their own, and they don't understand that it's going to take a long time, that there's already a lot of content available. So take that content, study it and evolve.

An interesting suggestion within this principle is related to the first two recommendations described in Principle 15. Remember I said that we have a lot of documentaries and films available on the market today? If you like history, it's very important that you watch documentaries like Chernobyl and Trotsky, which were true stories and in a few hours you'll understand a lot about these historical events and even beyond. From these two documentaries, you'll understand the rise of the Soviet Union and the fall of the country. I have an interesting thing to say about this, which is that by understanding the rise and the end, it will open up curiosity to understand the middle - which is why I took the two series, one that talks about the beginning and the other about the end.

My aim here is to help you evolve by starting simple. I'm giving you tools so that you can start right now. Another interesting point: if you want to understand a little about the life we live today and you like an action movie, you can watch a series like Peaky Blinders, which, despite being about the story of a gang, tackles issues of history, geography, politics, social movements, religion, all in a single series that portrays the daily life of real life at a given time.

My question to you is: doesn't that interest you? What are you waiting for to dive into this whole world that is available to you? Because I assure you, remember when I said that I've had contact with many millionaires and even billionaires? The culture of most of these people is very advanced. I, for example, who like to study history and wars, have watched a series called Band of Brothers a few times, which is very interesting and portrays some of the conflicts of the Second World War. I've probably seen every movie available on the subject, so imagine how much information it has given me about history, geography, other geopolitical issues and everything else. "Well, Charles, but I don't like any of this, any of these subjects", so you need to get out of this childish life of not liking anything. I'm not your mother who's going to feed you the last five spoonfuls of soup.

If you don't have access to any streaming service, be it Netflix, Amazon or HBO, there are plenty of programs on YouTube that are open to you. Like TED, for example, on various subjects. So, unfortunately, you have no excuse not to evolve in this area.

In this area of cultural expansion, the role of parents is also fundamental, because when they expose their children to quality information, they ensure that they have a good cultural foundation. For example, I grew up with little money but a lot of culture, and that has made all the difference to my life. I remember that my grandparents had always traveled a lot, and one of my mother's favorite things was to take us to the airport to see them off.

They always brought us some kind of present and I thought it was incredible. I'm talking about the 1980s, early 1990s, when my grandparents went to China, Japan, destinations that weren't so common at the time. They always brought back some kind of hat, paintings, and I thought: "He's gone to China, what a crazy thing to do"... so that sparked an interest in me. And it was also a house full of books, I mean, if you're reading this book and you have children, remember, all these habits that you're starting to acquire, of reading, of evolution, of watching documentaries, somehow all this will pass on to the next generations, as well as the negative things. In the same way that a father who drinks, couples who fight, you pass on aggression, even if it's not in front of your children; good habits also pass on and I'm only here because I'm the fruit of that, because I grew up looking at shelves full of books, and somehow that touched me. It's not a guarantee that it will work, but it's a very strong impulse.

This is essential, because parents who evolve greatly increase their child's chances of evolving (I've already talked about this here when I mentioned Bill Gates, computers and three hundred students). Parents who evolve certainly help their children evolve. What kind of human being do you want to be? What kind of father do you want to be?

17

Principle

Seek evolution and discover why millionaires don't have a million

We're coming to the end of this book, and I hope you've already understood that your actions will speak much more than anything else. My dealings with millionaires have shown me some very curious things, such as the fact that I've never met a millionaire with a million. Let me correct that, I've never met a millionaire with just a million.

Millionaires usually have more than a million and, with the life experience I've acquired today, I now understand why this is the case. The person who strives to have a million and works to reach their first million, breaks barriers, has discipline, is committed, evolves, seeks culture and everything I've been talking about throughout this book. Those who pursue this and reach their first million never stop. The good news for you is that success and growth are cumulative. If you've already watched the series I've been talking about, taken notes, looked after your health, if you've started taking the measures we've been talking about here since the beginning of the book, you're already a better person and, from now on, you'll only get better.

When we start to evolve, we're unlikely to want to involute, we'd have to make an effort to do so. So what skills did a person need to achieve in order to reach a million? Technical knowledge, a different mindset, new habits... As well as having reached a million, this person already has all the knowledge to do so, which makes it much easier for them to grow. It's also common for people to have become millionaires after their forties or fifties and by the time they die they've amassed a huge fortune, because the difficulty lies much more at the beginning than in the middle or at the end.

Getting out of the situation you're in now is much more difficult at the beginning than afterwards, when you just have to keep moving forward. Of course, you may be thinking of names of people who have lost all their assets, who have had difficulties in life, but in this book we don't look for the exception of the exception, we work with the average, and, on average, millionaires don't just have a million, they have much more than that. "Oh, I had an uncle...", fuck you. What we have to focus on is the average.

On this point, it's worth noting that we're talking about people who have become millionaires and then lost everything, and yet it's very common for them to get back on their feet. Have you ever stopped to think why these people manage to get back on their feet so easily? Simple, because they have already learned, understood and already have the tools to get there, so they need to repeat it, and repeating this process takes less time than acquiring all the learning.

Therefore, the chances of you prospering and evolving by following what I'm sharing here are enormous, with one advantage: evolution and learning are cumulative and are things that no one can ever take away from you. Every step you take here will take you further. And then it will take you further and further. Then you'll start earning money, and that money will provide you with culture, knowledge and feedback, which will bring you even more possibilities. So all you have to do is get started and keep going. Believe me.

It's also worth saying that I'm putting all these questions at the end of the book because, by now, you have to have understood all the advice to understand this key point. If you keep going, have discipline and all that, the chances of you reaching a million and then growing are much greater.

The big problem is that people are stuck in the surf. If you've ever been to a beach, you know that to get into the sea you have to go over the edge; sometimes it's very difficult to get over the edge, but then the sea gets calmer. Most people stand in the surf. You're in your job and you're promoted, but you have to work too much, then you leave, you fight with your wife... you're stuck because life is one big cliff. It's the same principle as the orbit: you can't get there at first, but once you do, it's much easier to multiply everything because you already have the toolbox and the knowledge you need to do so.

This principle also relates to the concept of "money attracts money". A person who has already passed through the valley of the shadow of death to get to where they are now will find it much harder to go back, unless they fuck up badly.

What can I do for you? Exactly what you need right now, at this early stage, to become a millionaire. People like to talk a lot about the first million, but to get there you need to change your mindset. If we're talking about millionaires, we also need to talk about mentality. The famous mindset.

Unfortunately, topics like mindset and coaching have been misused and misinterpreted in recent years, but they are concepts that we need to address here. After all, how are you going to be a millionaire if, in your mind, being a millionaire is a dirty, ugly thing, from people who aren't honest?

So let's talk a little about this mentality. It's not the main theme of the book, although I'm even thinking of tackling it one day in another book, but if you don't like millionaires, the chance of you becoming one is very slim, why? Because your mindset, your mentality is stagnant, it's programmed to dislike something. So, unconsciously, you'll be sabotaging yourself all the time so that you don't hang out with people like that and don't become people like that. Right?

I really like coaching, for example, and I even went to an event by the famous American coach Tony Robbins. I follow his work a lot, as he was a pioneer in this field. However, there are obviously people in this market who are not serious, just like in all other markets. That's why it's very important that, now that we're coming to the end of the book, you abandon some ideas that aren't going to take you forward. This mentality of not liking millionaires is very bad; how did it start? Well, it always starts the same way for everyone, that is, at home, with the family. Your mother telling you that your rich uncle isn't honest, that money is a dirty thing, that rich people don't go to heaven, the story of the camel and the needle, that it's easier for a camel to pass through the eye of a needle than for a rich person to enter the kingdom of heaven... This has all been working in your unconscious, so you can even tell me: "No, Charlão, I don't think that", but your unconscious does and it needs cleaning up.

An important aspect in this context is also the energy of money. I'm not going to go into that in depth in this book, but money is also about energy. So be careful not to dam up things in your life. If you have a lot of objects that you don't use, clothes, cutlery, old things, think carefully about turning this wheel. Find a way for your things, make the money turn. As it goes, it will come back, and maybe even multiplied.

There are many questions about money and mentality that, from now on, you should dedicate some of your time to understanding. Otherwise, you'll spend a lifetime wondering:

"Why do some people have money and others don't?"

I can't tell you why some do and others don't, but I can tell you for sure that those who do have a different mentality from the others. It starts in our head and, if it starts in our head, why are you taking action without changing it in your head first? It doesn't make sense, right? The reality is that it's much easier than it looks. I'm not asking you to start working eighteen hours a day from tomorrow; I'm just asking you, right now, to change your mindset, because working eighteen hours a day without changing your mindset will continue to make you poor.

Success is cumulative, because it is a constant evolution.

18

Principle

✻

Beware of your main enemy: the ego

This is the last principle, so if you've made it this far: congratulations! But there's a small problem that I still need to bring up for you... The idea is that you evolve more and more in your life, but when you start to evolve, a trap appears along the way: the ego.

In Judaism, we learn to deal with the ego a little bit, it's part of our history and culture. It's something we talk about, in other words, it's not a hidden issue. That's why we're aware that it can be a problem if it's not discussed. So the best weapon we can have against excessive ego is precisely the knowledge that it can be a problem.

Obviously, the ego has to be considered, at least in part. It is important, but it is also essential to understand the etymology of the word. The word "ego" comes from Latin and means our "self". So you have to think about yourself, right? Throughout the book, subjects such as self-responsibility, self-knowledge, a series of themes that deal with our inner knowledge, have been dealt with. So you've already understood the importance of focusing on yourself, but the problem arises when we take it too seriously. One of the characteristics of the Jewish people is to make fun of themselves. This in itself is an antidote to the ego. It's about not taking yourself too seriously.

The first fundamental point of this principle is to understand what the ego is. Ego is "I". Ego is the central, core part of someone, in other words, the core of the individual's personality, the individual's concept of themselves. The question, which we'll look at next, is when it can consume you to the point of going to your head.

I learned how to deal with this problem from an early age, because I'm part of the Jewish community and because I was taught this in my family. I'm part of a people that has practically been wiped out; they want to eliminate us all the time and we even joke about it, in other words, there's humor. The sad thing is that people take themselves too seriously. Still on this subject within Judaism, even on festivals we make a point of remembering bad times. You may have seen that at a Jewish wedding we wrap a glass and break it during the ceremony. Why do we do that? There are various theories, but the best known is that this way we remember, in a moment of joy, the destruction of the holy temple. In other words, even in a moment of joy we remember that sadness also exists and that there are also problems. This is like a thread that ties us to something bigger, so that we don't travel so much in the world's situations.

When a child is born, circumcision takes place on the eighth day, which is called brit milah. This is a moment of extreme joy in which we fulfill a covenant with the Creator, and there is also blood. So, in Judaism, we have joy and blood, we also have celebration and destruction and that's what keeps us connected to life. You can't go on a journey, you have to be centered and remember who you are, where you came from, the problems you've faced.

You may be reading this book and think you'll never suffer from this problem, but I don't know anyone who has prospered and who hasn't encountered it at some point.

Of course, I know people who haven't prospered, who didn't have the money, who weren't well-off and who also had problems with their ego. But, for example, in the ⍰⍰ years of work in which I've visited thousands of companies and businesses, most of the ego problems I've encountered have been with successful people. What's more, many times people who had come from nothing, from very low, would rise and become unbearable people, and why? Ego. They thought too much of themselves, that they were the center of the universe.

So it's no coincidence that this is the last principle in the book, because you're probably going to come up against this issue if you're successful. It's practically impossible, you have to be a saint, a very spiritual person to have money, to have status, to look in the mirror and not think that you are more than you are, that you are more important than people. It's very difficult, even more so in this world of influencers, and I say that with propriety, because it's a challenge for me too.

Sometimes our ego makes us so blind that we neglect or are too hard on our own families. To illustrate, I'll tell you a well-known Jewish story. There was a very successful man who had an elderly, sick father with Alzheimer's and various health problems. This man was very uncomfortable having his father at home, because he had to look after him. Until one cold winter's night, at dinner, the father dropped food on the Persian rug in the house. The son was very upset and snapped at his father: "Damn it, my Persian rug! You've made a mess! What will they think of that?" He continued: "My rug... Dad, you dropped it, so I'm going to leave you out in the cold for a while so you can learn."

This time, the old man's son turned to his own son and said: "Go and get the blanket for your grandfather because he's going to stay out in the cold for a while to learn not to do these things". Then the boy went upstairs to get the blanket and never came back, never came back. The father was already nervous about the whole situation, so he went upstairs to see what was going on. That's when he saw that his son was cutting the blanket in half, so he said to him: "Hey, why are you cutting the blanket? Give me the blanket so I can give it to your grandfather to keep outside". He replied: "No, Dad, calm down. I'm cutting up the blanket because half of it I'm going to give to Grandpa and the other half I'm going to keep for when you get like this too.

The moral we can draw from this story is that we have to be careful how we treat others, because we are replicating this to the world, and it has a way of coming back.

Now that we have some context about the ego, I'll explain how you can protect yourself. First of all, be responsible and know who you are. Exercise your self-knowledge, which we've already talked about a lot during the first principles. You need to have a clear definition of who you are and who you want to be in order to avoid problems with the ego.

An inflated ego leads to blindness and a lack of perception of reality. Always be aware of the ego's traps.

Beware of excessive self-regard, adoration and self-esteem. How many people lose themselves because they think they are better than others? According to the book The Ego is Your Enemy by Ryan Holiday, the ego is an unhealthy belief in one's own importance. I really liked this definition, and it explains why people who become famous with movies, soap operas, social networks, and who become rich think they are too important, and this also relates to what I said about Judaism. When I'm making fun of myself and not taking myself seriously, I'm already balancing this ego.

Ego has to do with your vanity or overvaluation. It's you for you and by you. Purpose, on the other hand, has to do with mission, with legacy, with what you do not out of vanity, but to help others, it's something bigger. In this way, the antidote to ego problems lies in the tripod: self-knowledge, mission and legacy. So before you ask me, I'll tell you how to solve the problem. Those who have a mission and want to leave a legacy don't focus on themselves all the time. Those who are self-aware know their problems and will try to protect themselves from this habit of thinking about themselves all the time.

If I know who I am and where I want to go, nothing will change my perception of reality. Beware, too, of a lack of humility; beware of thinking you're the best and have nothing more to learn. At every moment, in everything that happens to us, we can learn more, evolve and become better and better people.

When I worked with thousands of companies and entrepreneurs, I came across many of them who surrounded themselves only with people who agreed with them and were there to applaud them. This may sound good, but it can be very damaging. I've visited more than a thousand businesses in my life, and many of these successful businesses were run by successful individuals who, over time, surrounded themselves with people who applauded and agreed with everything. And if you're surrounded only by people like that, the chances of it going wrong are enormous. That's because everything you do is good, everything you say is good, everything you touch is better. Who can shield themselves from that? You won't be able to shield yourself and evolve if everyone around you is pulling your leg and clapping their hands.

The solution to this issue is to go back to a stage before that, where you're not just surrounded by people like that; in other words, you're supposed to hang out with normal people, people to whom you'll ask an opinion and someone in the group will reply: "That's a shitty idea of yours". Now, if you only surround yourself with applauding people, you get used to being arrogant if someone disagrees. So, in this case, the arrogant person asks for an opinion, but if questioned replies: "Who are you to question my idea? Who are you to question me? Look how much you earn. You're my employee, how can you question me?". And sometimes it's a guy who's at the cutting edge of the business.

Have you ever heard of people who detach themselves from reality? One example is people with an over-inflated ego. You can't surround yourself with people who will only applaud what you say. That's the ego speaking louder and louder. We can learn from everyone and at all times, as long as we empty ourselves of our ego, our arrogance and put ourselves in a position of humility, of learning. This is called life long learning.

I've read a few things about this, which is the concept of acquiring knowledge and skills throughout your life. We're never ready; if you've climbed one step, it's not over yet, there's another. Then you might ask me: "Don't you find that a bit tense? Doesn't it cause agony? Do we always have to go up a step?" I didn't say that we always have to go up, but that we are always learning. I'm not here to cause you anguish, just to encourage you to be better and better.

I like to see life as a blank book in which we are always learning and adding knowledge, with no limit to the number of pages. Therefore, the person who says: "Who do you think you are? Who are you to question me?", it's as if their book is closed, because there's nothing more to learn. The problem is that this is stupid because your ego is preventing you from going further, which is the concept of life long learning, where you are constantly learning.

There are people in their seventies and eighties learning new things every day, even more so with the internet. I've already mentioned several times here, during the book, that geographical barriers have fallen and that it's now possible to learn anything from anywhere. So what's the point of looking at something and saying: "I don't need that, I already know enough"? Who says you know enough? And even if you do know enough, listen, because there might be something in it for you.

Now I'm going to talk about my experience. How do I shield myself from it? By trying to keep my feet on the ground. Naturally and artificially. I force myself to keep my feet on the ground. How? I'll give you an example: imagine I'm going to the United States right now, and I can afford a first class return ticket; I can afford luxury hotels, but I decide to go first class and come back normal. I'll stay in good hotels and I'll stay in average hotels. Why am I doing this? Because I don't want to lose sight of the reality of people traveling, for example. Just as here in Brazil I still take the subway. People joke: "Aren't you afraid of taking the subway?". I say that I can't lose the concept of walking down the street normally, taking the metro, talking to people. You can't distance yourself from the reality that surrounds us.

I know people from my social class who question me about this and criticize me, because they think it doesn't make sense to be rich and not live like a rich person, that it's a poor person's mentality. No. This is a way of keeping in touch with people's reality. How can you understand anyone's life if you don't go to the supermarket to do your shopping? "Oh, Charles, so I need to go to the supermarket every month?". No. But you need to travel in a normal category, take the metro, do your shopping, you need to have a normal life at least once in a while. If you don't use some of these resources, you're too out of touch with reality. And that's bad even for business. Because it's important to have a sense of what real life is like.

There's another important point to make, which is one of Brazil's major problems in relation to politics, and that is the fact that politicians live in Brasilia, deputies, senators, ministers, and lead a very different life from the rest of the population. The guy leads a rich life, with a house, good health, security, he flies around in a jet and then you don't understand why things don't work properly for the population. It's very easy to see why this is, because their lives are very far removed from people's realities. When you're out of touch with reality, you lose track, and it all has to do with ego. That's because, if they really wanted to solve the problems, they should do as I said and armor themselves, get down from where they are to where things are happening, and understand what life is like.

Be aware of this, when you realize that you're only focused on yourself and your reality, drop the ball, put your feet on the ground, remember where you came from, don't be conceited, work hard, be humble, always be open to new knowledge and learning, be honest with yourself, with your flaws, qualities, respect yourself and respect others, challenge yourself, be with people who provoke you, don't move away from them because otherwise you'll become unanimous and all unanimity is stupid. Get together with people who think outside the box, who have something to add, who think differently.

It's important to have a diversity of opinions because when you only have one idea, you can't evolve to another side. There's a saying: "Two Jews, three opinions". That's because when you put more than one Jew together, everyone has a different opinion and there's an argument, and it's exactly about thinking differently. If everyone thinks the same, how do we develop? The ego gets in the way, it numbs you, it makes you neglect the basics because it deludes you with the fantasy that you've already reached the top, and we believe that the top doesn't exist. And yet a phrase says: "We are nothing, you are still very small in the face of the magnitude of the world and the divine".

Another point related to politics is that ego can lead you to corruption, because once you think you're better than others, smarter, more prepared, more astute, more effective, more clever, you think you won't get caught. You end up not having this block of fear. Why aren't we corrupt? Firstly, out of conviction, often; and secondly, out of fear. If you don't have this fear barrier because you believe that nothing will happen, you weaken yourself. Problems with the ego can also lead to corruption.

For example, what helped me a lot to lower my ball was to acquire self-knowledge. Always maintain sobriety, normality in your life. Don't get carried away with success. Don't get carried away with your achievements, as we said at the beginning of this principle. Be clear about who you are and who you want to be. You'll need this to protect yourself.

The ego can destroy you, so you have to watch out for it at all times. And one way to protect yourself with others, for example, is very simple: admit you made a mistake and apologize. Now that you know that the ego can create pride, that you can often become an unmanageable person, you will protect yourself against it. So you need to start apologizing immediately when you make a mistake. Ideally, you shouldn't make mistakes, but if you do, apologize. And try not to interrupt people from now on. If you say something and someone wants to debate it, just listen. One of the things that can help you with your ego is to listen more. You're not perfect, you fail, you make mistakes, and the beauty of life is that you learn and evolve from that.

Having said all that, try not to create fantasies about yourself. We're human and it's in our nature to project the things we want. I myself talk about projecting, what car I want to have, what house I want to buy, the quality of life I want to give my family. However, I'm telling you not to try to project yourself like a superhero. You can project the good things in life, and this is a healthy practice. "Wow, I want to have that house in five years' time", nice. But projecting that you're someone you're not, and someone you shouldn't even want to be, is wrong. Get it? Everyone knows an asshole boss. The big problem is that most people want to be that boss and end up becoming an asshole too.

The ego can also cause a major problem: not evolving. Why don't you evolve? Because you don't ask for help, because you think you're too good. How many people do I know who have stopped studying, taking a course or something because they have that "I already know things" on the tip of their tongue? Then you'll have a block.

If your ego is inflated, everything goes down the drain, because you start feeding unhealthy parts of yourself with the resource of money. And the fall is great. We can see this in relation to social networks, for example. There are influencers who grow, gain millions of followers, but start lying because they don't want to stop feeding their ego in a disordered way. I even know the case of a blogger who claimed to be vegan, then she became ill and, due to her lifestyle, was forced to change her diet. The problem was that she didn't tell her followers and started doing everything in secret. Obviously, in the case of a person with millions of followers, someone is going to find out. People found out and she was forced to tell the truth. But the question is: why didn't she tell the truth? Ego.

There's another similar case of a blogger who had gained a lot of muscle mass. He claimed that he didn't take any kind of supplement, until it was discovered that he did. Why didn't he tell the truth? Ego once again. So the same force that makes people go up also brings them down, because as we go up in terms of career, money, everything, it's as if someone is pumping up your ego. To shield yourself from this, you have to make a hole and let it empty, have an escape valve.

It sounds a bit contradictory, but it's important to think about the "I", the ego. The only problem is how much you're thinking only about yourself.

As I've said a few times in this book, it's important to know yourself, to know your origins, where you came from and, above all, where you want to go. Now, what's wrong with knowing a lot about where you come from? You don't always come from a nice place, but you know where you want to go. You don't change where you come from, but you often come from a nice place, you have to remember that too. If you didn't come from a nice place, you can project where you want to go. If you know these parts of yourself, or at least one or the other, it's hard for the ego to get to you, because you connect with your mission. Well, if I want to be a great financial educator in Brazil, transforming the lives of thousands of people, but I treat someone with arrogance and I'm a jerk to them, that's it, there's no more mission or purpose, there's nothing.

Self-knowledge favors this. It's almost impossible to find someone who has self-knowledge, has been through a lot of problems, but has self-control, knows their mission, their purpose, and has problems with their ego or bullies everyone. Well, if someone has all this, but is arrogant, then they really don't have a mission, purpose or value. They're lying. That's why I say it's essential to know our history and who we are.

As I said at the beginning of this book, I had a very important family reference: my grandfather. He gave me a lot of cultural baggage. But if I didn't, I'd project where I want to go anyway, and that attitude would help me. However, there are many people who come from a broken home, and that's where the importance of reframing lies, which is part of the process of self-knowledge.

There's a book called In Search of Meaning, which became well known because the author lived in a concentration camp, and there he came to the conclusion that anyone who lost the meaning of life died. It was such a hard life that if you didn't have any meaning, if you didn't think about your family, you wouldn't survive. That's why there are reports of people who were even attached to a job. For example, a man who chopped wood in a concentration camp. Just by attaching yourself to the meaning of it, you stayed alive. But when you gave up that sense, you died of something like starvation. It's important to note that these people ate a hundred, two hundred grams of food a day; two hundred grams is enough calories for a guy to stay alive like a stick, but those who had a sense lived a little better.

There's another story, which doesn't belong in this book, but it's about a mixed concentration camp. There was a man who always saw the other man working well, happily, helping everyone a lot, and he thought that was strange, especially in a concentration camp. Everyone was being beaten, there was nothing to eat, but that man worked happily. He watched that guy and thought: "Fuck, how does that guy manage to have that kind of attitude here, in a place with all this barbarism, with everyone being murdered and so on, and he still manages to help others?". So he started observing the guy and discovered that, every morning, he would take a bag, go into the bathroom, stay for five minutes, and come out of the bathroom with the same bag. He kept looking at this situation until one day he decided to approach the guy: "Hey, I notice that you behave differently here, and I've also noticed that you go into the bathroom every day for five minutes, stay alone and come back. What's going on?". And he replied: "I'm a Lithuanian general who was arrested here in the war with you. But when I was arrested, I asked to be allowed to bring my uniform. So every morning, I take my uniform into the bathroom, put it on, look at myself in the mirror for five minutes and remember who I am. I'm not a prisoner who's alive here, I'm a general in Lithuania. I'm much more than that. I will survive. So I feel different.

This is a fucked-up story because, even in the most difficult moment of his life, living in a deplorable reality in which people were being killed right there, that man didn't change his behavior. He knew who he was. That's why, even if you're in a bad situation, it's important to remember who you are, where you came from and where you want to go. One situation I've experienced a lot, and I think it fits in with this, is when you lose your job. It's so hard to lose your job that you don't want to go out, you don't want to meet anyone, you don't want to go to family events... After all, everyone will ask you the same question: "Have you got a job yet? How are you doing? Have you seen that opportunity? What about that website? Have you seen that ad...?". Sometimes people even want to help, but that's not what's really going to get you back on your feet.

Returning to the question of legacy, there are still people who don't necessarily have to think about it, and yet manage to control their ego. I'll give you an example, there are people who don't have time to think about legacy; sometimes the guy has just got married, has two children, is full of bills to pay, wants to be promoted and still has to do an online MBA at night... This guy has so much going on in his life, so many challenges, so many problems, that he often isn't thinking about legacy. But a guy with a life like that probably won't have an ego problem either, because he's already being bombarded by things that will put him "in his place".

By now, we've come to the conclusion that everyone can have an ego problem, but it's usually a bigger problem for those who are getting on a bit in life and are surrounding themselves only with people who agree with everything. But then it's important to point out that it's not just successful people who have problems with their ego. Everyone knows someone who, even if they can't afford it, treats people badly and doesn't say "good morning" to anyone.

When you become successful, if you start to think about what kind of legacy you want to leave, that will prevent the ego from getting in the way. If I want to leave a legacy on Earth of financial education, free materials for people, with videos, books, with a series of benefits for the world, that will almost be a shield against the ego.

"Oh no, I don't give a damn about legacy. There's no legacy for me, I'm going to work like there's no tomorrow, I don't want to leave anything for anyone." Well, if you don't want to leave anything to anyone and you don't give a damn about everything, look how you're leaving a little door, or at least a window, open for the ego to get in your way.

If you pay attention to this tripod formed by self-knowledge, mission and legacy, it's practically impossible to have an ego problem. Because the ego, which would be the self, will be in the right place. You'll be thinking about yourself, but you'll be creating something positive, with a good intention. For example, I can't imagine someone leaving a positive legacy on Earth by treating others badly.

This principle comes last in this book precisely because anyone who has a lot of problems in life doesn't have to start this journey worrying about the ego. You'll start with self-knowledge, then self-responsibility, and then you'll go through a series of learnings before you get to the ego. Starting to think about the ego to solve the problems in your life is like a guy who has bought a plot of land, is thinking about building a house and the first thing he buys is the curtain. It doesn't make sense, because there are other things to look at first when building your house: there's the pillar, the brick, the mass, the foundations of the house...

I'm not saying that those who are in a more unfavorable life situation don't need to think about their ego. I'm not saying that. It's just that, normally, the more your life prospers, the more you're tempted and run the risk of letting it go to your head and suffering from selfishness.

Who do you think will have a bigger ego problem? Someone who is just starting out in life, starting to make money, thinking of getting married, or a successful businessman, with a financial empire, with several employees pulling his strings, with society on his back, known nationally?

You have to look in the mirror and remember that this situation is temporary, that it's not this situation that defines you.

It's obvious that you both have ego problems, but I'm not talking about the exception to the exception, but rather the rule. The rule is what we see most in people and, generally, the ego attacks people who deal with a lot of money. But worse than that, the ego mainly attacks those who don't have the self-knowledge to balance their "inner self".

Epilogue

Enjoy the journey. Of all the things I could record at the end of my first book, this is by far the most important.

When I began the process of writing this book, my concern wasn't with revealing the quickest way to the pot of gold at the end of the rainbow, in other words, the reward, which has become increasingly common amid the pressures of today's immediate world.

The idea of bringing you the eighteen principles you've just read was precisely to make you realize that the most essential thing when it comes to success is the act of enjoying the journey that takes us to the place we want to be.

For some reason we have been brought up to only celebrate when the final reward arrives, but as this happens people forget that in the whole process of searching for the reward there are several pots of gold along the way. When I was on the Camino de Santiago de Compostela pilgrimage, for example, I didn't cry compulsively when I arrived at the city's cathedral on the last day, but I cried several times along the way, because I enjoyed and experienced the whole journey. I loved that process.

That's why not paying attention to the beauty of the path causes us to stop loving the process, because we become inattentive to what's going on and desperately want to get rid of the problems that arise in the middle of the path, because then we only see ourselves in the eye of the hurricane. But although it sounds strange, many problems can be great opportunities that lead us to something much better.

In this book, for example, I've told you about my problem with being overweight, thirty kilos too many to be exact; I've told you about my problem with a great deal of dissatisfaction when I found myself without a job, without the personal and professional results I wanted to achieve, and completely frustrated. And as well as talking about the problems of more recent years, I told you how at the beginning of my adult life I was fucked out of money, having to drop out of college, only to return two years later with my class; and finally, I told you about the problem of getting into social media, having almost no views for practically a whole year, and yet continuing to do it, and seeking constant improvement. To give you an idea, when I started my podcast, only eight people listened to me. And yet I kept going. I kept studying, improving, asking what people liked, and two years later, twenty thousand people were listening to my podcast, we managed to reach the top of the list, being the Top 1 Business Podcast on Spotify in August 2023, imagine if I had given up in 2018.

In each of those phases of life when I encountered problems, I could have remained frustrated, complaining that nobody gives a damn, curled up in a fetal position and never got up, condemning my life to complete failure. But instead, I set off in search of what I could do differently to achieve the results I have today.

Returning to the example of the YouTube channel, when you start working with it, you discover a lot of problems that you had no idea existed, but then you start researching and see that other people have also gone through this, and soon you're solving them and it's happening. So when you finally reach 100,000 subscribers, you'll be celebrating a lot more than the person who only bothered to reach that mark.

When I opened the channel, like most people, it didn't go off straight away. But that wasn't a problem for me, and you know why? Because I simply decided to love the process. With every difficulty I overcame, new video I uploaded, quality of material I brought, even if it only had a dozen views, I felt happy and grateful. Having difficulties at first is terrible, but they will certainly make you much stronger.

And for those of you who have read my book, I'll say it again so you don't forget: you have to love the process, understand that all this is necessary and part of evolution. Do you know why? Because, at the end of the day, it's all about the journey. It doesn't matter whether the result of X million is achieved or not, because if it goes wrong you've learned a lot along the way. If you learn a lot during the process, you keep going, which means you don't stop at the first hurdle.

Loving the evolutionary process, that is, the whole journey we make in this world towards a purpose, mission, legacy, or simply living life in the best possible way, is the only way to enjoy the journey and finally give real meaning to everything we do.

Understand, therefore, that the journey is already the greatest reward. What's more, when we're doing what makes sense to us, we keep going at all costs, because we're living in the reward. An example of this is when we're in a company, where we spend a couple of years working, and then we get fired, but then we join another company that's even more fucked up and we get promoted. At this point we don't have to lament that our story didn't work out in the first company, but rather that our process there wasn't over yet. In fact, the process we have to go through doesn't necessarily have to be in one place, as it unfolds throughout our lives.

As we mature, we come to understand the relationship between time and why things don't happen at the speed or in the way we want them to. Now, the way we react to this will make all the difference, because what we saw back in our history as something that slowed us down can be a great lesson that has allowed you to move forward in a way you never imagined possible.

In closing, I'm not asking you who are just finishing this book to understand exactly everything I've said here, but I am asking you to think about these principles when things are going wrong. Is it really going wrong or is it just a change of course that is requiring you to have a different way of looking at things from now on?

The 18 principles you've just learned about aren't a laboratory test of your life; in reality, they've been tested in my life and I've also realized that they all happen in the lives of successful people, and they're even being consolidated in my own journey, because there's still a lot to happen in my life. But what I consider to be the most important has already happened for me, which consists of not wanting to understand everything, recognizing that things are part of a process, that I need to enjoy every moment of life, experience the journey and not just think about the pot of gold at the end of the rainbow, because the meaning of evolution lies in loving the process.

We often don't understand that having difficulties makes victory much better.

I hope you'll start incorporating one by one of the principles proposed here into your life right now, if you haven't already, and remember to follow them with discipline and consistency and, above all, enjoy the journey!

BOOKS TO CHANGE THE WORLD. YOUR WORLD.

To find out about our upcoming releases
and available titles, visit:

www.**citadel**.com.br

/citadeleditora

@citadeleditora

@citadeleditora

Citadel – Grupo Editorial

For more information or questions about the work,
please contact us by email: